Langston Hughes

Titles in the series Critical Lives present the work of leading cultural figures of the modern period. Each book explores the life of the artist, writer, philosopher or architect in question and relates it to their major works.

In the same series

Langston Hughes

W. Jason Miller

REAKTION BOOKS

Published by Reaktion Books Ltd
Unit 32, Waterside
44–48 Wharf Road
London N1 7UX, UK

www.reaktionbooks.co.uk

First published 2020
Copyright © W. Jason Miller 2020

Printed and bound in India by Replika Press Pvt. Ltd.

A catalogue record for this book is available from the British Library

ISBN 978 1 78914 195 5

Contents

Langston Hughes, February 1942.

Prologue

'Unfortunately, having been born poor – and also colored – in Missouri, I was stuck in the mud from the beginning. Try as I might to float off into the clouds, poverty and Jim Crow would grab me by the heels, and right back on earth I would land.'[1]

Langston Hughes dreamed of reaching the clouds. The central theme in his poem 'Dreams' (1923) declared: 'Hold fast to dreams', because without them, life is a 'broken winged bird/ That cannot fly'.[2] Epitomizing the Harlem Renaissance movement that peaked in the 1920s, Hughes represented the 'New Negro' of the era, calling for substantive economic and political changes for all African Americans.

The author answered to several names: poet, journalist, playwright, novelist, editor, translator, librettist and short story writer. As he moved from home to home as a child, and then travelled around the world, he enjoyed extended residences in the USSR, Mexico, Spain, Italy and Paris, and he wrote much of his most famous poetry while abroad. Writing most nights from midnight until dawn and then sleeping in past noon, Harlem, New York, eventually became his umbilicus. In 'I Dream a World' (1941) Hughes's revolutionary idealism imaged change on a global scale: 'I dream a world where all will know/ sweet freedom's way.'[3] As the optimism of youth gave way to the cynicism of middle age, Hughes saw the central aspirations of his race as a 'Dream Deferred' (1951).

In what became his most recognizable metaphor, deferred dreams 'dry up like a raisin in the sun', or worse, '*explode*'.[4]

As the first writer to bring the blues into poetry, Hughes became a symbol to all dark peoples of the world. The most translated American poet throughout the Hispanic world, he directly inspired others, such as Cuba's Nicolás Guillén. At home, every African American author to follow owed something of their career to his success: Hughes was the first black author in America to make his living exclusively by writing. However, despite composing an astonishing sixteen volumes of collected works in his lifetime, he never became rich. As such he accurately characterized himself as a 'literary sharecropper tied to a publisher's plantation'.[5] By the 1950s Hughes came face to face with what it meant to be labelled 'subversive', falling under FBI surveillance and intense scrutiny when Joseph McCarthy called him to testify on television about his communist sympathies. Mystery surrounded his sexuality, with men and women each vying for his affections.

Hughes called as many musicians his friends as he did writers, moving easily through crowds where Duke Ellington, Billie Holiday, Ada 'Bricktop' Smith and Harry Belafonte exchanged smiles with Zora Neale Hurston, Ralph Ellison, Richard Wright, Alice Walker and Gwendolyn Brooks.

Signing his name with his trademark green ink, the inside covers of gift books captured his efficiency and innovative style as he crossed the 't' in Langston and started the 'H' in Hughes with one swift motion. His cheerful generosity made him beloved by children, and he was so popular he appeared in advertisements selling Smirnoff Vodka during the late 1950s. Just as he had done by reading his poetry in tandem with jazz decades before it became a trend in San Francisco and Greenwich Village, Hughes redefined the American theatre by featuring gospel music in his plays. The man with nearly sixty books to his name was friends with photographers such as Henri Cartier-Bresson, and advocated for

Marion Palfi and Roy DeCarava. He even offered a groundbreaking photo-text – understanding how photography and poetry could work symbiotically.

By the end of his life, in the 1960s Hughes had become a cultural ambassador to Africa, introducing Nigerians to the smooth jazz of Lionel Hampton and spending evenings abroad with Russian poet Yevgeny Yevtushenko. Hughes's poetry had a direct impact on the civil rights movement and the rhetoric of the most recognizable dreamer of all: Martin Luther King Jr. Before he passed away in 1967, Hughes had travelled to Nigeria with the civil rights leader, who consistently incorporated his poetry into his public addresses, and he answered an earlier letter to write an unpublished poem at King's personal request.

1

Motherless Child, 1901–19

Raised believing freedom was something you fought to win, Langston Hughes was brought up by his maternal grandmother Mary Langston in Lawrence, Kansas. The nearly seventy-year-old woman, whose own mother was Cherokee, left her home in Fayetteville, North Carolina, for Oberlin, Ohio, after men attempted to enslave her at the age of nineteen. Quite symbolically, James Langston Hughes was born on 1 February 1901, nearly sixty years before the Greensboro sit-ins started and Black History Month's official inception. It was only recently discovered that his birth year was actually a year earlier than had been previously believed by everyone (including Hughes himself).[1]

Named after his father, whom Hughes hated, his first name was quickly abandoned. Jim Hughes was a frustrated businessman who had two white fathers in his bloodline. His rushed marriage to Carolina 'Carrie' Langston in 1899 amid rumours of a 'shotgun wedding' eventually resulted in their infant child dying of unknown causes.[2] Leaving Guthrie, Oklahoma, months before their only other child was born in Joplin, Missouri, the couple's frequent moves throughout the Midwest set in motion a life of travel. Hughes led a blues lifestyle, learning early on that home was a place you left.

The writer would state: 'My theory is that children should be born without parents – if born they must be.'[3] Hughes felt this way as his own father left immediately after he was born on extended trips to Buffalo and Cuba before settling on his own for good in

The almost seventy-year-old Mary Langston, *c.* 1910, around the time she was raising Hughes in Lawrence, Kansas. Not only had Mary fled North Carolina in her youth when men tried to enslave her, but she inspired Hughes with her stories of real-life heroism, including the death of her husband Lewis Leary as he fought with John Brown at Harpers Ferry in 1859.

Mexico. Though trained as a teacher, Hughes's mother Carrie was forced to relocate away from her child as she took odd jobs as a maid or janitor while longing for a successful stage career that never materialized.

Hughes came from a family with a very storied past. The roots to his family tree are so tangled that it is often difficult to distinguish which branch each one feeds. His grandmother Mary would place a shawl over young Langston as he slept at night, reminding them

Langston Hughes, age three, around the time he started sleeping under a shawl he believed was worn by Lewis Leary when he died.

both of the rich heritage of their ancestors. Langston was told that the shawl had been worn by Mary's first husband, Lewis Sheridan Leary, who died with John Brown at the raid on Harpers Ferry. The nine-year-old Hughes was filled with awe at the story of the valiant attempt to free slaves when he saw his grandmother seated with distinction at a dedication ceremony where President Theodore Roosevelt spoke.[4] Mary's second husband, Charles Langston, had halted fugitive slave John Price's return to the South in the very public 1858 Oberlin–Wellington rescue. Excelling while breaking conventions, John Mercer Langston, Charles's younger brother, not only had a city and college in Oklahoma named after him, but was the first vice president of Howard University and served as a Virginia Congressman in 1890.[5] Charles Langston's father Ralph Quarles had lived with former slave Lucy Langston as man and wife and they are buried as close as custom allows, still facing each other on opposite sides of a segregated cemetery.

Carrie came and went. When she was back at home, she took her son to see plays such as *Uncle Tom's Cabin* and *Buster Brown* in places as far away as Kansas City, and Hughes developed his love of theatre from her.[6] It was in Kansas City where he heard his first

Carrie Hughes Clark, *c*. 1925, was often working and returned to win key battles that kept Hughes in school, even as she dreamt of a theatre career that never came to pass.

blues: a performance by a blind orchestra where the music 'seemed to cry when the words laughed'.[7] Well before he transposed them into new poetic forms, he wrote down many of the songs he heard, and some would inadvertently be attributed to him as poetry he himself wrote:

I'm goin' down to de railroad, baby,
Lay ma head on de track.
I'm goin' down to de railroad, babe,
Lay ma head on de track –
But if I see de train a-comin',
I'm gonna jerk it back.[8]

Working about 96 kilometres (60 mi.) away in Topeka as a stenographer for the black-owned and -operated newspaper the *Plain Dealer*, Carrie sought to briefly enroll her son under her own care for his first year of school. Her uncertainty about where he might attend school – Topeka, Lawrence or even Mexico City – may be the reason she shared his birth year as being later than it actually was. Making the extra year known might have resulted in either her or her son standing out in unwanted ways. When Langston was sent across the tracks to the segregated school, she argued with the white school principal and won (four decades before the city would become famous for *Brown v. Board of Education* in 1954). Before Carrie returned him to Mary's home in Lawrence and headed off to work in Colorado Springs, Langston endured hearing his first teacher tease the children that they should not eat liquorice because it would 'make you black like Langston'.[9]

Life with Mary Langston included stories from the Bible, hymns, *Grimm's Fairy Tales*, and every newspaper and magazine she could afford. She told him stories of Haitian heroes while he sat on a stool or 'stretched out on the floor, staring up at the stars'.[10] Her work as part of the Underground Railroad and education as one of Oberlin

College's first African American students left him hearing 'tales of heroism, of slavery and freedom, and especially of brave men and women who had striven to aid the colored race'.[11]

When Mary died in 1915, Langston lost a woman whose eyes were as wise as an owl's. Whe he was fourteen, he went to live with close family friends, James and Mary Reed, a couple he knew before his grandmother's death. With Auntie Reed, Hughes drove the cows, set the hens and ate 'wonderful salt pork greens with corn dumplings'.[12] Often sporting a chequered flat-cap on his head and wearing knickerbocker pants, he found that eating from their garden was a substantial improvement over the dandelion greens Mary had served. The poet probably conflated the two women when he wrote 'Aunt Sue's Stories':

> Aunt Sue has a head full of stories.
> Aunt Sue has a whole heart full of stories.
> Summer nights on the front porch
> Aunt Sue cuddles a brown-faced child to her bosom
> And tells him stories.[13]

Hughes starting delivering newspapers at about the age of thirteen. Pages of the *Saturday Evening Post*, *Lawrence Democrat* and the leading socialist weekly in America, *Appeal to Reason*, arrived in mailboxes and doorsteps from the hands of Langston Hughes.[14] While delivering papers would be a common first job for many, the activity must have held special meaning for Hughes as he would eventually both write news articles sent from the Spanish Civil War and have his own weekly column in the *Chicago Defender* for more than 22 years, where he used humour as a weapon to attack racism in every form. More people read Hughes's newspaper columns during his lifetime than his books of poetry.

Seventh grade in Lawrence also provided another formative experience. When his teacher segregated the few black students

Langston, *c.* 1910.
Often seen delivering
newspapers around
Lawrence, young
Langston grew up in
mostly white schools
and neighbourhoods,
accepting work such
as cleaning out brass
spittoons.

in the class, Hughes created cards that read 'JIM CROW ROW' and placed them on each of his black classmates' desks. When the teacher challenged him, he ran out onto the school grounds, repeating over and over that his teacher had a 'Jim Crow row'. Summarily expelled, community leaders joined his mother in getting him reinstated with one significant change when he returned: the classroom no longer had any Jim Crow row.[15]

Hughes, in 1915 at the age of fourteen, took a lowly job at a white hotel where he worked for 50 cents a week cleaning the lobby. The work included the task of cleaning out the 'Brass Spittoons', something Hughes would put into verse: 'Clean the spittoons, boy', where 'the smoke' and 'the slime' become 'Part of my life'.[16] Whatever humiliation he felt in such degrading work, it prepared him for the jobs he was to take later when he sailed the world in his twenties as a deck-hand. More importantly, cleaning never compared to the pain he felt after a decisive church revival gathering; believing he would literally see Jesus, as his Aunt Reed said he should, only young Langston and a friend remained unsaved at the front of the church. When the friend walked away only pretending to be changed, Hughes was all alone, unable to fake the experience he was sincerely expecting. Stone still, he eventually answered two questions when the preacher agonizingly approached and was thereby hailed as 'converted'. That night he wept anything but tears of joy. He felt he had lied, been lied to and, worst of all, that Jesus had passed him by, not caring enough to appear before his waiting eyes.[17]

Hughes never forgot this painful experience at Aunt Reed's St Luke's African American Episcopal (AME) Church. Yet it did not inhibit him from writing numerous religious plays, especially during the last two decades of his life in Harlem when storefront churches, the rise of the 'Social Gospel' and gospel music compelled him to attend St Philip's Episcopal Church so often 'they considered him a member'.[18] In Hughes's play *Tambourines to Glory* (1963), the characters of the two Reed sisters evoke the faith of both Mary

Reed and her husband James, her curious opposite who 'would have been deemed a foil to his saintly wife'.[19] Throughout his life, Hughes was never considered religious as his 'evasiveness about his own faith was consistent with other "identities" he seemingly disavowed or disclaimed'.[20]

Carrie Hughes married Homer Clark in around 1915, and the two took Hughes to Lincoln, Illinois, for a formative eighth-grade year. Joined by stepbrother Gwyn, Homer's work in the steel mill contrasted sharply with a title Hughes would claim shaped him as a writer: 'Class Poet'. According to Hughes's autobiography of 1940, 'my classmates, knowing that a poem had to have rhythm, elected me unanimously – thinking no doubt I had some, being Negro.'[21] One of his teachers remembered Hughes differently as 'standing intellectually head and shoulders above the group'.[22] Long after he delivered his class poem publically at graduation, Hughes's poem 'Genius Child' (1937) captured these tensions when he wrote '*Nobody loves a genius child*'.[23]

Homer Clark quickly tired of the heat of the mill and took to the rails, working as a conductor in Cleveland. Carrie, Gwyn and Langston arrived in the city at 11217 Ashbury Avenue just as Homer bolted for Chicago. When his mother and stepbrother left to join Homer, Hughes lived alone, surviving on money his mother sent or brought back on brief visits to Cleveland. Hughes would remember surviving on rice and hot dogs throughout the next four years. Poor, black and alone, he was 'reading Schopenhauer and Nietzsche, and Edna Ferber and Dreiser', remembering that it was 'de Maupassant who really made me really want to be a writer'.[24] At Cleveland's Central High School, Hughes suddenly found himself popular, serving as student council representative as well as secretary, treasurer and president of several clubs. His best friend Sartur Andrzejewski was representative of a school made up mostly of children of Eastern European and Russian immigrants, and he lent Hughes copies of two communist publications, *The Liberator* and

Langston with Homer Clark, Carrie Hughes Clark, Gwyn 'Kit' Clark and a friend during his eighth-grade year. Taken in Lincoln, in March 1916, this is just before Homer moved to Cleveland, only to leave again for Chicago once the rest of his family joined him.

Socialist Call. It was here that Hughes was first drawn to a new writer in the pages of the radical magazine *The Liberator* named Claude McKay, a man whom he would always admire, even after surpassing his achievements in letters.[25]

In fact, Hughes even went and heard the socialist leader Eugene V. Debs speak, celebrating the Russian Revolution of 1917 with many of his classmates.[26] As a result, he was called into the principal's office to explain why he attended, while many of his classmates faced more serious repercussions, such as having books removed from their homes by the police.[27] Seeds of what would flower before and beyond his most radical period of the 1930s were sown when Hughes found in Russell and Rowena Jelliffe a married couple whose support would exceed even that of the Reeds. The Jelliffes had started a community centre in Hughes's neighbourhood that came to be known as Karamu House. Hughes started teaching art classes there to young and underprivileged children. As such, Hughes started spending time with them in their home and leaned on their emotional support.

Winning the city relay in his junior year, Hughes poses here in his high-school track outfit without any hint that he is actually living alone in Cleveland.

Though he helped the school track and field team secure the city championship during his junior year by running his leg of a winning relay, Hughes managed many holidays alone, too poor to afford the letterman sweater that other teammates wore. This was a poverty he spent the next thirty years unable to outrun. For now, he spent his time wearing jackets without chevrons and reading the poetry of Walt Whitman, Carl Sandburg and Paul Laurence Dunbar.

He wrote his first story based on a newspaper account of a poor white maid named Mary Winosky, who nonetheless died with more than $8,000 to her name (nearly $122,000 today).[28]

Hughes's childhood – whether in Lawrence, Lincoln or Cleveland – included growing up in nearly all-white neighbourhoods. Though an unexpected beginning for a writer who would earn the unofficial title 'Poet Laureate of the Negro People', he had negotiated racism perhaps all the more often, sometimes taking a 'blow to the jaw' when visiting Chicago to see his family and winning protests against segregation in his classrooms.[29]

While in Cleveland Hughes left behind his best friend Sartur to attend a dance at nearby Longwood High. Andrzejewski wanted to remain a 'bachelor' forever, and the two men had formed a 'strong, intimate connection that was quite possibly sexual'.[30] Writing about their own personal connection, Andrzejewski would pen the words: 'There are a great many things we feel we ought to say to each other. We needn't. We shall always understand, though others may never.'[31] However, when Hughes saw Susanna Jones at the dance, he immediately felt how one jewel can outshine a whole gym full of dresses. Unlike the mostly white girls Hughes sat with at Central, she had a face 'like an ancient cameo/ Turned brown by the ages'. His attraction and jubilance continued:

When Susanna Jones wears red
A queen from some time-dead Egyptian Night
Walks once again.[32]

Hughes finished his poem 'When Sue Wears Red' (1923) by declaring that something ancient and as old as Egypt had arrived; a new form of beauty that Hughes completely admired. Having written a poem that he was proud of, he turned giddy with joy. Only a high-school junior, Hughes was already on the verge of writing the most important poem of his career.

2

I, Too, Am America, 1919–24

Hughes found himself travelling by train to visit his father in Mexico after graduating from Central High School in Cleveland in May 1919. Back home he would part his hair to the left, but travelling meant hiding as many racial markers as he could under a hat. This would not be the same trip as the summer before, when he was accompanied to Mexico by his father, a man who photographed like a Mexican outlaw. That three-month stay was eventful in all the wrong ways. During that trip, the young Hughes had seen at first hand his father's hatred of those among his own race who stayed behind in America to accept racist treatment and poor wages. He had also endured a tense confrontation with his father when he overslept early one morning for a trip he hoped would allow him to see his first bullfight. Suffering a remarkably odd reaction to his father's verbal abuse, Hughes's anxiety (and silence) combined to leave him so debilitated he ended up in a hospital wheelchair with an unidentifiable illness. Worst of all, Hughes had gone so far in contemplating suicide that he would later write: 'I put the pistol to my head and held it there, loaded, a long time, and wondered if I would be any happier if I were to pull the trigger.'[1]

On 20 July 1920, Hughes was once again in the midst of returning to Mexico – alone – hoping missed bullfights and suicide attempts were behind him. His destination was Toluca, where his father lived, not far from Mexico City, and Hughes had travelled along his normal route, making the turn south from St Louis,

A man Hughes always feared, James Nathanial Hughes, *c.* 1930. James moved to Mexico to escape racism in America after bestowing his only son with his own birth name. It was a confrontation with James that led Hughes to contemplate suicide in 1919.

Missouri, finding himself in the heart of Texas. He was journalling, heading the page of his notebook: 'A Diary of Mexican Adventures (if there be any)'. In his small, top-ringed notepad, he noticed 'red flowers singing their colors along the track' and 'reliving the monotony of ever green landscape and always cotton growing, cotton growing'. Then, only three sentences in, he documented more personal events: 'Being in Texas I am not allowed to forget my color.' The only 'Negro' on the train car, Hughes told of having a white man leave the table because he did not want to eat with him. Later he documents the stares of disapproval he received. Hughes then begins to explain how he 'passed' for Mexican, as he would continue to for years to come to avoid danger. He wrote of covering up his 'curly' hair and then speaking enough Spanish to secure a private berth to Laredo.[2]

The most important aspect of the entire trip had already occurred. Crossing the Mississippi River near St Louis, Hughes had reached for a letter from his father and written his most famous poem on its envelope. 'The Negro Speaks of Rivers' is the third published poem of Langston Hughes's career. Having cultivated a relationship with editor Jessie Fauset, who had already accepted several of his poems for *Brownies' Book*, a collection of works for children, Hughes sent her this more serious piece, which she placed in *The Crisis*, the leading African American journal of the age, in June 1921. The poem has become synonymous with how Hughes achieved canonical status: 'I've known rivers ancient as the world and older than the flow of human blood in human veins./ My soul has grown deep like the rivers.'[3] The poem's 'I' has been understood as an archetypal figure who has absorbed collective knowledge across the divide of time while the addition of the word 'Speaks' in the poem's title reflects the long oral traditions of storytelling. Hughes's rhythms in the final line above create a tone of solemnity through its anapaests. While 'soul' has denotative associations with one's eternal spirit, the more relevant understanding of the word activates something more difficult to define. More contemporaneous meanings of the time help to read it as a race consciousness that is shared with others only after being deeply internalized. As Hughes himself would say, soul is 'a sort of synthesis of the essence of the Negro folk arts . . . expressed in contemporary ways'.[4]

The poem references universal racial experiences going back to the waters of the Euphrates, the shores of the Congo and pyramids along the Nile. The Mississippi River that the poet experienced becomes a point of reference: where Abraham Lincoln saw the injustice of slavery and where Hughes now has the courage to bask in the sunset. Blues musicians knew that to even mention the name

'Mississippi' conjured great fear, and sunset was a time where mobile blacks were thwarted with signs that read: 'Nigger, don't let the sun set on you here.'[5] Despite his fears of lynching, brought to him through the often sensationalized stories in Negro newspapers and *The Crisis*, which he had read since his youth, Hughes found a way to reassure himself by writing a 'meditative lyric that contemplates the way in which African Americans have previously survived and flourished near riverscapes'.[6] When Hughes looked, he saw that the boulders in this river had more value than mountains.

It was a riverscape that reminded Hughes of what it meant to be sold downriver, the dangers he himself would face passing through Texas looking for adventures, and it would claim an unmistakable poetic connection with Walt Whitman, whose own poetry also offered free verse built on anaphora. The word 'speaks' in the title conceals this, asserting that an oral framework is sustaining the poem, but it is Whitman's influence that provides the form. Hughes's love of Whitman surpassed that of nearly all other poets, except perhaps for Carl Sandburg.

To understand just how exciting Hughes's free verse appears, the poem must be compared to the metred and rhyming stanzas that were in vogue in 1921. Hughes's lines read as if they were four decades ahead of the era, as most poets were assimilating to European standards. Representative of this fact, take 'My Race', published in *The Crisis* five months after Hughes's poem:

My life were lost, if I should keep
A hope-forlorn and gloomy face,
And brood upon my ills, and weep
And mourn the travail of my race.[7]

Leslie Pinckney Hill's quatrain above was not merely accepted by the magazine; the poem was an excerpt from the author's published book *Wings of Oppression* (1921).

Later, when the poem was collected in book form in 1924, Fauset was probably picking up on the reference to 'soul' throughout the poem when she asked Hughes if he would like to dedicate it to the magazine's esteemed editor (and her secret lover) W.E.B. Du Bois, whose master work was *The Souls of Black Folk* (1903). Hughes gladly consented. He continued to support Du Bois, writing a newspaper article in 1951 that aided in his acquittal on charges of aiding a foreign government.[8] His affections for Du Bois were genuine throughout his life. Even when it eventually became too dangerous to write publicly about Du Bois' politics, he instead wrote to the great intellectual privately in 1956, confessing that he had just finished reading '*Souls of Black Folk* for the tenth time'.[9]

The poem would not only serve as the centrepiece of Hughes's poetry collected in anthologies, it also took on a greater life of its own. Marian Anderson sang an arrangement of the poem, including at her farewell concert in Carnegie Hall in 1965.[10] Hughes eventually pitched an unsuccessful film idea under the same title, and when Hughes's body was cremated, it was this poem the mourners recited as his body was wheeled away.[11] The poem has inspired others in different ways.

Hughes had written this poem on his way to Mexico, spurred to visit by his father's vague offer to send him to college. Having left Langston and his mother, perhaps in no small part because of a contemporaneous lynching that occurred near where Hughes's train had just passed in Joplin, Missouri, James Hughes had become a successful businessman in the fifteen years since his arrival. He owned a ranch, sheep and cattle, and though his worth fluctuated, his real-estate investments had allowed for a staff who grew to tolerate his tirades and accept his brand of discipline. Thanks in no small part to this trip, Langston fortuitously missed a horrific adventure that could have cost him his life. While out of the country, a young girl named Herta was over visiting with the family housekeeper Bertha Schultz. The recently widowed brew master whom Herta worked for stormed in and shot the girl three times, then shot Schultz in the arm. The man's anger stemmed from the fact that he erroneously suspected Herta of having an affair with Langston. Both women miraculously lived, but with Hughes himself being the true source of his ire, it is doubtful he would have survived had he been there.[12]

When Hughes's one-year stay in Mexico came to an end, in mid-August 1921 he sailed to New York City, having stubbornly won an argument with his father to attend Columbia University. Earlier that summer his father had laid out his wishes for his son to study abroad in Switzerland or Germany, then return to Mexico as a mining engineer.[13] Informing his father of his dislike of mathematics, his desire to write, and then showing him his recent publications in *The Crisis*, James Hughes consented to fund one year of study at Columbia. Hughes would later explain that he chose Columbia because he '*really* wanted to see Harlem'.[14] Even as a youth, Hughes told how he would 'go down to the railroad station in Kansas and touch the sides of Pullman cars that had come through from Chicago and say to myself Chicago isn't so far from New York'.[15] Travelling by boat to the mecca of his dreams, Hughes arrived in New York city on 4 September. His father would survive a stroke the next year, permanently losing the use of his right arm, but Hughes would not return to nurse him. In fact, as the next year saw their relationship disintegrate, the two men never saw each other again.

Hughes experienced a frustrating year at Columbia University. Beyond feeling bored by his professors and excluded by his classmates, Hughes's angst had started immediately, when he had to argue for his room at 111 Hartley Hall.[16] Unable to distinguish from his application that a 'Negro' had applied from Mexico, the university was ill prepared to welcome him. In fact, only three years later students would burn a cross outside of Furnald Hall to 'smoke out a black resident'.[17] His assignment for the school newspaper *The Spectator* was a farce as he was assigned the fraternity beat when none of the few African Americans on campus were allowed inside Greek housing. Befriending a Chinese student, who also introduced him to Chinatown, Hughes submitted a few pieces to the school's newspaper under the name 'Lang Hu', as if to highlight his anonymity and the fact that no one knew 'who' Langston was.[18] Hughes quit his studies after his first year.

For Hughes, leaving Columbia did not mean losing Harlem. He took odd jobs – first on a vegetable farm and then delivering flowers. He attended shows at the theatre that featured such works as *Shuffle Along* (1921), a barrier-breaking production with an all-black cast that helped launch the careers of Josephine Baker and Paul Robeson.[19] Harlem was just beginning to emerge into the dream it would become, and Hughes was there to see it all starting to take form. Hughes's signature metaphor of the dream had already appeared in his earliest poetry. 'Fairies' (1921), the first poem he ever published, begins, 'Fairies weave their garments/ Out of the dust of dreams.'[20] In one of his most quoted poems, 'Dreams' (1923), he declared the importance of clinging to one's hopes: 'For if dreams die/ Life is a broken-winged bird/ That cannot fly.'[21]

With 'The Negro Speaks of Rivers', 'Negro' and 'Dreams' standing among his most revered poems, Hughes would write another classic into the canon with 'Mother to Son'. Published in December 1922, it is not clear if memories of his grandmother or his experience with an optimistic Harlem landlord named Mrs Dorsey inspired the poem.[22] In lines that may reflect the spirit of both women, Hughes began: 'Well, son, I'll tell you:/ Life for me ain't been no crystal stair.'[23] The woman speaker then lists the obstacles that have tried to keep her from climbing up. In the end, she combines commitment and force so that the young man listening will likewise not give up. Following her lead requires a determination that she models everyday by moving ahead in spite of barriers that would cause others to quit. The poem became deeply embedded in the common vernacular of African American culture. Lorraine Hansberry's landmark play *A Raisin in the Sun* (1959) had the working title of *The Crystal Stair*. Coretta Scott King recited this poem from memory on stage at the end of the famous 1965 march from Selma to Montgomery led by her husband. As late as 2011, Oprah Winfrey spoke these lines from memory on camera when climbing the steep section of a bridge in Sydney, Australia.[24] With more references than can be named, Hughes recognized the success of speaking through the voice of female wisdom.

Hughes was genuinely inspired by the encouragement of Jessie Redmon Fauset and was soon introduced to a man who might have become his nemesis, Countee Cullen. However, the twenty-year-old poet and Hughes admired each other, attended the theatre together and exchanged drafts of works in progress. Cullen had one man in particular he thought Hughes should meet, and Professor Alain Locke of Howard University followed with his own admiration for Hughes. Cullen probably considered Hughes naive, which may have lessened any humiliation felt by Hughes spurning his subtle advances; however, Locke was more persistent. Before Hughes would fully distance himself from each man, he first stepped into a Harlem nightspot where something of his love for the blues was sparked.

Though he had heard the blues during his Kansas childhood, and would only later truly realize the music's significance during his time hearing performances in Paris, Hughes was first drawn to write about it in March 1922. Without using the crutch of punctuation, he began this poem with a virtuosity that captured the hesitations of delivery that featured so prominently in the medium: 'Droning a drowsy syncopated tune'.[25] Two things conspired to keep him from publishing 'The Weary Blues'. First, he had more problems ending the final lines of this poem than any other he would ever write; second, Hughes immediately realized the poem was exceptional, so he hid it from everyone until it was ready, even Cullen.[26]

Turning down an invitation to travel overseas with Cullen and Locke, Hughes set out on his own journey, understanding to some degree the desires each man held to be intimate with him. On 13 June 1922, Hughes actually left dock on the *West Hesseltine*, passing the lighthouse at Sandy Hook for the shores of Africa. Arriving in the first of 32 ports (spanning Dakar and Senegal) Hughes apparently joined the sailors in Lagos, Nigeria, when they went into the bordellos, and he was also alone with at least one crewman onboard, as throughout his life he would share intimacies with both men and women.[27] Startled, Hughes realized that 'The Africans looked at me and would not believe I was a Negro.'[28]

Citing his lighter skin colour, and what he called his grandmother's Indian hair, Africans saw his 'mulatto' features as a barrier. Though he was a smooth-lipped negotiator, even as he approached the age of 22, his lighter skin tones left him looking out of place. As such, he was greatly disturbed when he was refused access to a drumming ceremony, being informed that the god being honoured by the ritual would not 'tolerate the presence of a white man'.[29] Hughes would continue to carefully note how race was merited as he travelled throughout his life. In a journal he kept from his 1930 trip to Cuba, Hughes noted ten different labels for race including 'Indio' and 'Mulato'. He noted that *blanco* meant 'light', *la caneta* was equivalent to 'colored' and *negro bembon* was similar to 'nigger', noting also the significance of hair in determining such labels.[30]

Hughes would highlight his mixed background on many later occasions to undermine the logic of racism in America. Noting especially that he had white foreparents, Hughes was willing to accept neither African nor American standards of blackness. At the time of his first trip to Africa he would write a poetic statement that reads like an anthem of the 1960s Black Arts Movement:

The night is beautiful
So the faces of my people.

The stars are beautiful,
So the eyes of my people.

Beautiful also is the sun,
Beautiful, also, are the souls of my people.[31]

'My People' (1923) asserts the primacy of choosing one's racial
heritage when faced with cultural constructs of race. Moreover,
it employs the logic espoused by African standards against itself,
selecting natural beauty rather than blackness as the marker of
unity. The colours black, white and yellow are implied in each
of the images of night, stars and sun, as if Hughes is enumerating
precisely how he is united, with each of the three people groups
that such colours symbolize. Finally, nature itself is the measure
of elevating the black body to standards whiteness cannot refuse.
If white male heteronormative values of nature's night, stars and sun
are undeniably beautiful as American ideals stated in the first lines,
then each of the poem's second lines reveals in calm tones how the
smiling speaker's race shares the exact same features. The poem
asserts that anyone who values the beauty of nature cannot refute
the black body, whose skin, eyes and radiance share the natural
world's same qualities. A world that is elevated and adored must
surely accept human beings who possess its same beauty.

Returning to Harlem with a monkey named Jocko in tow,
Hughes was welcomed by Cullen into the rising excitement of a city
in the throes of rebirth. With novels by Jean Toomer in circulation
and others such as Jessie Fauset's *There Is Confusion* (1924) underway,
Hughes deferred his attendance at Howard University under the
guidance of Locke and headed straight for Europe. Seeing a full-
page spread of his poems in *The Crisis* did not delay him as the

McKeesport set sail for Holland.[32] Once there, Hughes abandoned the voyage and took a train to Paris. After hailing taxis as a doorman in exchange for his dinners, he eventually ended up in Montmartre, where, thanks to Rayford Logan, he worked as a dishwasher at Le Grand Duc. Though this was early 1924, Hughes did not move in the same circles as American expatriates such as Ernest Hemingway, F. Scott Fitzgerald or Gertrude Stein. Instead, recounting it all in entertaining fashion in *The Big Sea* (1940), he was working all night in a café that featured the jazz vocals of first Florence Embry and then Ada 'Bricktop' Smith. Eventually, another café different from where Hughes worked, Chez Florence, was named after Embry, a woman Hughes described as being famous for her 'unattainable aloofness'.[33] In the very heart of it all, before she herself became the wealthy owner of several jazz clubs, Bricktop was consoled by Hughes when she had her purse stolen along the pier, with him assuring her that she too could live off nothing as he had upon his arrival in Paris: seven dollars to his name and yet 'I was still living.'[34] He observed violent fights between Chef Bruce and the owner, one even settled at knife point. Eating only coffee, Hughes confessed in a letter to Countee Cullen: 'For a week I came as near starvation as I ever want to be.'[35] As a mere dishwasher he benefited from a clever trick: the waiters received commission for how many bottles they sold each night. Crafty waiters lifted near-empty bottles from patron's tables as they delivered full ones, then held the takeaways in reserve so the entire staff could drink champagne for breakfast. With even hot water scarce for someone on his budget, Hughes advised Cullen: 'stay in Harlem . . . the colored jazz bands and performers are about the only ones doing really well here.'[36] Yet seeing black art revered beyond America slowly reaffirmed Hughes's commitment to creating his own brand of modernism, by celebrating what the larger world already welcomed.

Hughes soon found himself reciting the work of his favourite black poet Claude McKay with Anne Marie Coussey, a brown-skinned English woman with a large inheritance awaiting her back in London. The Jamaican McKay's poem 'Spring in New Hampshire' (1920) had brought the two so close that the English Coussey proposed to Hughes, three months after they first met in March 1924. Some combination of Anne being cut off from her allowance by her father and Hughes's own reticence left them separating on good terms but without so much as a final kiss.[37] Changing many names on legal advice from his lawyer, Hughes would mildly disguise the relationship when he wrote of 'Mary' in his first autobiography. Writing two poems documenting their affection, 'A Letter to Anne' (1927) and 'Breath of a Rose' (1940), the latter suggests 'Love is like perfume' and 'Love is no more/ Than the breath of a rose.'[38]

Two months passed until Locke himself informed Hughes that he was on a summer trip through Europe. Still interested in attending Howard University, Hughes joined the university professor for remarkably insightful tours of museums from Paris to Italy. While Hughes would greatly exaggerate his plight about being stranded in Italy when he wrote in *The Big Sea* of being robbed of his wallet and passport, the reality was that he willingly loitered peacefully without Locke for six weeks in Genoa. Suggesting in print that he instead tried to reach Claude McKay in the south of France, Hughes actually relaxed during days that were 'as pleasant as anything I can ever remember'.[39] Though a patient and faithful friend, Locke would not recall their departures in quite the same way, writing to Hughes: 'I have opened my arms three times to you, closed my eyes in confidence, – and waited. And three times, I have embraced thin air and blinked and then stared in disillusionment.'[40]

His funds dwindled in Genoa as he sipped wine, read and wrote what would eventually become his most translated poem. 'I, Too' (1925) offered a strong corrective to Whitman's 'I Hear America Singing', and Hughes signalled that even the open-hearted Walt Whitman had been deaf to the voice of dark Americans, instead cataloguing only the country's carpenters, masons and mechanics.

```
          I, TOO


I, too, sing America.

I am the darker brother.
They send me to eat in the kitchen
When company comes,
But I laugh,
And eat well,
And grow strong.

Tomorrow,
I'll sit at the table
When company comes.
Nobody'll dare
Say to me,
"Eat in the kitchen,"
Then.

Besides,
They'll see how beautiful I am
And be ashamed,-

I, too, am America.
```

Langston Hughes

Autographed copy of 'I, Too' (before line nine was later changed in 1959 to 'I'll *be* at the table'). Little did Hughes know how important this poem would be as he sent a copy for Alain Locke to publish in *Survey Graphic* and then *The New Negro* in 1925.

In his poem, Hughes declared that the black servants who are currently ushered into the kitchen would one day sit at the table themselves, 'strong' and 'beautiful'.[41] The work soon took a place of privilege, recited to end the poet's readings throughout the South in 1931.[42] Hughes's dreams of what equality would look like tomorrow was titled 'Youth' (1924). It was also sealed in an envelope addressed to Locke as Hughes boarded a ship bound for America after ten months away. Europe had been its own education, and Harlem was still waiting for him when he returned with memories of Paris.

Hughes spent 10 November 1924 as the guest of Countee Cullen at a function for the National Association for the Advancement of Colored People (NAACP) that felt more like a homecoming for one of the city's most beloved authors. He would meet Walter White, James Weldon Johnson, Arna Bontemps and Carl Van Vechten for the first time. Though Van Vechten would soon become regarded as the 'Tastemaker' of Harlem, his first introduction foretold nothing of the great importance he would play in shaping Hughes's career as he went home and scribbled that he had met 'Kingston Hughes'.[43] But where some relationships sparked, others ended. Bontemps and Van Vechten would soon become Hughes's closest friends. However, Cullen may have imagined the level of Hughes's intimacy with Locke and become frustrated by such illusions given that his poetic peer had refused his own sexual overtures. Cullen and Hughes would soon part ways, each silent until the end about exactly what divided them.[44]

3

A Bone of Contention, 1924–30

In order to know a place, you have to leave it. Through his connection with Alain Locke, Hughes still hoped to attend Howard University in Washington, DC, and took an opportunity to live nearby with his cousins. While Harlem had called to Hughes, and would remain his umbilicus, he instead found himself spending fourteen months in Washington, DC. The city's upscale LeDroit Park did not suit him, so he left his relative's home for more humble accommodations. Arriving back from Italy with only a quarter in his pocket, Hughes bounced between odd jobs at a laundromat and an oyster restaurant before accepting work from Carter G. Woodson. Under the distinguished professor, who would eventually pioneer Negro History Week, Hughes was responsible for everything from dusting, posting letters and preparing the furnace day and night.[1] He also alphabetized the 30,000 entries for Dr Woodson's book *Free Negro Heads of Families* (1925). The activity was dull and mind-numbing: each name was on a separate sheet of paper waiting to be manually sorted, one by one, as if six hundred decks of cards needed stacking from ace to king. In sharp contrast to Harlem, Hughes found Washington representative of two contrasts: 'ghetto life' or the upper class of successful blacks that he considered 'unbearable and snobbish'.[2]

Even though he was not in Harlem, the city was about to define Hughes. When Jessie Fauset invited him to an occasion she said he could not miss, Hughes borrowed the train fare from her, fought through the malaria (which he had contracted in DC) that had sent him to bed for ten days, and arrived for the 1 May 1924 *Opportunity* magazine awards banquet on Fifth Avenue. It was the 'greatest gathering of black and white literati ever assembled in one room'. With every major publishing house represented, James Weldon Johnson stood up to announce, and then recite, the winning entry for poetry. Hughes's 'The Weary Blues' had triumphed over 703 entries to claim first prize.[3] With Countee Cullen, Zora Neale Hurston and Aaron Douglas present, all of Harlem now knew the name of Langston Hughes as he walked away with $80 when an anonymous donor matched the prize money. The term 'Negro Renaissance' was coined the next day, when the title of the story covering Hughes's triumph graced the pages of the *New York Times*. There was no doubt that a new movement was in full swing, and from that moment on it would be forever associated with Langston Hughes.[4]

Though they had met briefly the year before, Carl Van Vechten now took special interest in the winner. With genuine interest and pure motives, the white 'Tastemaker' of Harlem took an exhaustive number of photographs through the coming decades to document black artists. He would fight to establish the famous James Weldon Johnson collection at Yale University, where Hughes's exhaustive papers are available to scholars. Van Vechten's love of jazz was legendary, and he was more interested in its 'black roots, as opposed to its white branches'.[5] Van Vechten arranged a meeting with Hughes and asked for a collection of his poetry, and with personal conviction about the verse he advocated with his substantive clout to Blanche Knopf for a book. Eighteen days after winning first place, *The Weary Blues* had been accepted for publication. A delighted Hughes proclaimed: 'I'll have to walk sideways to keep from flying.'[6] Van Vechten would become Hughes's most trusted reader, receiving every first manuscript from him for the next 24 years.

Busboys make good poets, and when Hughes switched jobs again to work at the Wardman Park Hotel in Washington, DC, he was doing both jobs at once. Hughes was making $55 a month, while being close to the kitchen and the food he took from it for free, and writing during his time off in the afternoons. He received proof pages for his book and worried that its illustrations reduced people to caricatures.[7] In November 1925, he seized upon a chance to connect with a poet beyond Harlem's orbit: when Vachel Lindsay – then one of the most prominent poets in the country – came into the restaurant the day of his own scheduled poetry reading, Hughes left handwritten copies of three of his own poems beside his plate. Muttering something about his respect for Lindsay before scurrying away, Hughes woke the next morning astounded to learn that Lindsay read all three of the poems at his event, declaring admiration and praise for the hotel's 'unknown' author. The next day reporters asked Hughes questions, took pictures and placed a story run by the Associated Press up and down the East Coast.[8] With his white uniform, his hat pulled down, his ears shot out as if he had just paid for a haircut, Hughes revealed an awkwardness towards his new-found fame. Continually harassed, he was forced to quit the hotel, but with his first book of poetry set for release just six weeks later, the timing could not have been better.

Hughes read poetry to music well before it was popular three decades later in Greenwich Village and San Francisco. He demanded that a true blues musician be present at his 15 January 1926 reading at the Playhouse in Washington, DC, only to be annoyed when Locke snuck in a refined player who communicated black bourgeois values. Striking black and red tones framed a piano player on the dust jacket of *The Weary Blues*, and these bold colours were just the right wrapping paper. Hughes had given a gift of music that even 'Father of the Blues' W. C. Handy responded to enthusiastically, calling it an 'entirely original' work.[9] He was now giving readings accompanied by musicians such as Fats Waller.[10] He knew the blues deeply, having collected hard-to-find lyrics that even impressed folklorist Alan Lomax, who wrote that

A visit by poet Vachel Lindsay inadvertently thrust Hughes into the spotlight as writers and photographers flocked to document the undiscovered 'busboy poet' who worked in Washington, DC, at the Wardman Park Hotel in 1925.

Hughes's version of 'Dupree Blues' was 'the best he or his father have come across'.[11]

In bringing the blues into the genre of poetry in *The Weary Blues*, Hughes came to embody the world's image of a black writer. In some ways, Hughes was riding the wave of interest in blues music with the first phonographs of the genre having just appeared in

1923. Interest in Hughes's engagement with this music eventually inspired Steven Tracy to bring attention to it, and others such as David Chinitz have advanced this rich vein of scholarship. Not merely creating poems about jazz and the blues, or printing ones he had heard performed, he created a new form of poetry. Hughes actually wrote 'blues poems' that include the creative addition of literary devices. Only this coalescence allows the blues to be effectively placed in print. He started with simple typographical tricks to communicate the oral nature of performance. Hughes's 'Homesick Blues' (1926) works to show how words slur when he writes: 'Homesick blues, Lord,/ 'S a terrible thing to have.'[12] The repeated line that follows instead reads 'Homesick blues is', to serve as visual evidence for how the 'S' is simultaneously connected to 'Lord' the first time, and then overtly enunciated as 'is' when the blues repeats an idea with variation through signifying.

Receiving his first payment from *Vanity Fair*, which paid him 50 cents per line in 1925 for three new poems, Hughes opened a cheque for a scant $17. As a result Hughes started to break the standard AAB lines of the blues into six lines rather than three, allowing him to make twice as much money in the future. This economic decision also resulted in more spaces for him to insert literary devices.

With his first book of poetry just released, Hughes also took centre stage in the era's most important anthology. With the Negro Renaissance now a named movement, Alain Locke gave it a bible when he turned March's special edition of *Survey Graphic* magazine into October's anthology book *The New Negro*. While Locke's anthology codified the role of these writers as 'anti-capitalist militants', its title has been rekindled often throughout scholarship as a means to recapture the importance socio-economics played during the era.[13] In the end, the period offered more than a simple flowering of art: it revealed a desire to change the political power and class status of all African Americans. Though never intimate,

Locke and Hughes had been corresponding ever since their time in Italy, and little did the poet know just how important his missives would be. 'Youth' and 'I, Too', sent directly to Locke for his consideration, became part of the twelve poems included in *Survey Graphic*. Moreover, these would also serve as the basis of the eleven poems featured in *The New Negro*. Locke singled out 'Youth' in his introduction to the anthology as the type of verse most representative of the current generation of Harlem writers, allotting Hughes more poems than any other poet. Hughes represented what the New Negro wanted.

When Locke was fired for demanding an equal pay scale for white and black faculty and trying to remove mandatory chapel services for students, Howard University was suddenly no longer an option for Hughes to accept without this mentor's presence there. An eight-day student strike did not save Locke's job, even after thirteen years of service, so Hughes considered Harvard because it held out the opportunity for a scholarship. However, an accidental meeting turned Hughes away from following the same path as Countee Cullen. Riding on a bus, Waring Cuney was reading an article about a black poet only to look up and see the man himself standing next to him. The two struck up a conversation, with Cuney espousing his personal love of Lincoln University. The campus of about three hundred students was located in Pennsylvania about 65 kilometres (40 mi.) from Philadelphia. With Amy Spingarn – a white benefactor who, among other things, sponsored the prize money for the *Opportunity* literary contest Hughes won in May 1925 – supplying his loan, and a lifetime of friendship after, Hughes enrolled mid-year, starting in February. Hughes immediately began acting rather debonair on campus, wearing a fedora hat bent down to cover his right eye and wry smile, his sheepskin jacket made him look as if he had just jumped elegantly off a slow-moving train. Though its faculty was all white, the university would educate some of the future's most legendary leaders such as the first black Supreme Court justice Thurgood Marshall, Nigerian Governor General Nnamdi Azikiwe and Ghanaian Independence leader Kwame Nkrumah.

Within weeks Hughes was commuting to Harlem for book promotion events and parties, where everyone from Salvador Dalí to Bessie Smith was likely to appear.[14] When they were not high-status events, such as the ones hosted by A'Lelia Walker, Van Vechten, Fauset, Aaron Douglas or Walter White, Hughes was hearing low-down versions of the blues that would never even have been broadcast on radios at rent parties. At such parties visitors payed a charge at the door to enter and hear the music, thus allowing the tenants to raise enough money to pay their landlords. Hughes attended 'one almost every Saturday night' in the summer of 1926, finding them often more 'amusing than any nightclub'.[15] Wallace Thurman, future husband to Louise Thompson Patterson, captured the personalities who attended these soirées in his novel *Infants of the Spring* (1932). Hughes, veiled as 'Tony Crews' in Thurman's book, was portrayed as 'close-mouthed and cagy' when it came to personal matters. He either had 'no depth whatsoever, or he was too deep for plumbing by ordinary mortals'.[16] The bisexual Thurman would imply he was 'more than just friendly with Hughes', but this boasting was not true.[17]

The magazine *The Nation* engaged the country in a debate that had still been left unresolved. Were African Americans to create their own art, or were they to assimilate to European standards? What were the implications of the choice? Which art would most legitimize the status of black artists and the culture they represented? On 16 June 1926, George Schuyler asserted in no uncertain terms that the world had 'patiently waited' for 'a great renaissance of Negro art just around the corner' to express the '"peculiar psychology" of the Negro'.[18] Hughes called Schuyler's idea an absurdity when the latter titled his article 'The Negro-art Hokum', and Hughes was personally

Handwritten copy of 'Youth' with alternative title 'Tomorrow' (1931). With this poem, Hughes became a symbol of what the New Negro wanted.

invited by *The Nation* to answer. A week later Hughes had penned the manifesto of the entire era when he wrote 'The Negro Artist and the Racial Mountain' (1926). Hughes did everything but name Countee Cullen in his first line. He wrote:

> One of the most promising of the young Negro poets said to me once, 'I want to be a poet – not a Negro poet', meaning, I believe, 'I want to write like a white poet'; meaning subconsciously, 'I would like to be a white poet'; meaning behind that, 'I would like to be white.'[19]

While the statement suggested objective artistic standards, Hughes used this idea to signal that writing white implied much more beneath the surface where morality, class, sexuality and upward mobility were interrelated. Hughes would codify a position that now seems inevitable to many when he declared that one cannot sacrifice roots for growth. Hughes made it clear that Africa, blues and jazz did not set a low bar for the next generation of African Americans seeking credibility. In fact, these were the new standards.

Hughes instead asserted that authenticity is credibility. No mere minstrel act, Negro artists were intent on honouring their past. Though Hughes's statement became the anthem of the era, Hughes was hardly alone in his stance. Aaron Douglas wrote to Hughes a year earlier saying that the two should create an 'art era' featuring something more than 'white art painted black', something out of 'material crude, rough, neglected'.[20] Moreover, one of Hughes's final images may owe something to W.E.B. Du Bois's statement in 'What Is Civilization – Africa's Answer' (1925)'. Written the year before, Du Bois had asked:

> What is African music? Have you heard the tom-tom . . . this ecstasy that of Fear runs that rhythmic obligato, – low, sombre, fateful, tremendous; full of deep expression and infinite

meaning; have you dancing in your soul and have you heard a Negro orchestra playing jazz? Your head may revolt, your ancient conventions scream in protest, but your heart and body leap to rhythm.[21]

Perhaps Hughes was thinking of the great intellectual's passage when he wrote:

But jazz to me is one of the inherent expressions of Negro life in America: the eternal tom-tom beating in the Negro soul – the tom-tom of revolt against weariness in a white world . . . the tom-tom of joy and laughter, and pain swallowed in a smile.[22]

Hughes realized people could present their self as a solid surface hiding inner desires. As such, he intended to melt anyone whose frozen depths allowed them to turn their mouths against the same images of low-down culture that their eyes could not resist. Hughes understood personally the role that class played, and he alluded to himself when he wrote of

a young colored writer, a manual worker by day, who had been writing well for the colored magazines for some years, but it was not until he recently broke into the white publications and his first book was accepted by a prominent New York publisher that the 'best' Negroes in his city took the trouble to discover that he lived there. Then almost immediately they decided to give a grand dinner for him.[23]

In the end, race was the metaphor that concealed so much more than it revealed. Activating the language of the Greeks, biblical mountains and freedom known by slaves, he ended his manifesto:

We younger Negro artists who create now intend to express our individual dark-skinned selves without fear or shame. If white people are pleased we are glad. If they are not, it doesn't matter. We know we are beautiful. And ugly too. The tom-tom cries and the tom-tom laughs. If colored people are pleased we are glad. If they are not, their displeasure doesn't matter either. We build our temples for tomorrow, strong as we know how, and we stand on top of the mountain, free within ourselves.[24]

If race was a mountain, you had to pass through it if you ever hoped to reach the top. Those who avoided it would end up walking a long circle at the same elevation they already occupied. Hughes was prepared to lose the decade in order to win the century.

Hughes's second book of poetry, *Fine Clothes to the Jew* (1927), received mixed reviews when it appeared. The collection suffered as a result of its odd title, one that many suspected Van Vechten had influenced (to be provocative). The title phrase was meant to headline a concept in the black community captured in the poem 'Hard Luck' (1926), of being so poor you 'sell your clothes' for money. Kind critics, the ones who sided against the Schuylers of the world, found that the book demanded readers to carefully 'distinguish clay from mire', and Claude McKay liked it even more than Hughes's first. Those who called it 'Hokum' included those who preferred verse that was less 'tawdry', and a *New York Times* review found it 'flawed'.[25] As for subject-matter, Hughes had stayed true to what he argued earlier. He refused to write about 'Vanderbilts' because at least 'two-thirds of all blacks were lower class'. He genuinely affirmed the greatness of blues singers like Bessie Smith, who were being 'honored in Europe'.[26]

Alain Locke, already responsible for including Hughes in his anthology *The New Negro*, now went further in promoting the poet when he introduced him to Charlotte Mason. At 72, and the wife of Dr Rufus Osgood Mason, this patron had much of the same motivation as Van Vechten to aid black artists. When she stood, she stared straight through her rimmed glasses. Wearing pearls around her neck, her silver hair was held in folds like a heron's wings at rest along the shore. Offering Hughes and Zora Neale Hurston an allowance, she saw her role of support as an opportunity to exert influence on literary history from her Park Avenue home, where a total of nearly a dozen artists (including Aaron Douglas) were accepting her support. With his solitary luxury up until then being securing the only single room allowed any student at Lincoln, Hughes thought carefully before accepting her $150 a month stipend. She was now his 'Godmother', the name she demanded as he began his first novel, *Not Without Laughter* (1930).

In a move that some regard as 'censorship', Hughes began writing his semi-autobiographical novel under the influence of Godmother.[27] This likely accounts for why Hughes said decades later: 'I loathe this book.'[28] However, in toning down (or even omitting) much of the intended social commentary on poverty present in his original drafts, Hughes's Depression-era book would still outsell all his other books released before 1938 and end up being translated into eight languages. In the novel, the blues itself seems to be a character, and Hughes worked to unify and blur traditional boundaries between the blues and gospel.[29] Aunt Hagar not only captures the biblical figure she is named after, but activates the '1921 blue's song "Aunt Hagar's Children's Blues" which was recorded over two dozen times by 1942'.[30] As he would do with nearly all his future dramatic works to come, Hughes also blurred the realm of poetry by incorporating it into prose. Hagar herself sometimes sounds exactly like the speaker in 'Mother to Son' when she exclaims several times that 'things is kinder hard'.[31] Young Sandy, who mirrors Hughes, takes inspiration from Hagar and is 'proud every evening of his six unblemished brass spittoons' cleaned each day of 'tobacco juice, cigarette butts, wads of chewing-gum, and phlegm'.[32] Hughes's own poem 'Brass Spittoons' (1926) was clearly upcycled here, and even his poem 'Red Silk Stockings' (1927) can be connected to the reactions Harriet gets when she auditions for a job at the carnival.[33]

By far the most interesting bridge between genres is an unpublished poem Hughes included in the original manuscript. Perhaps written while he stayed on after exams at Lincoln one summer, Hughes's 25-line 'Poem for a Dance' is written word for word in his novel.[34] Combining the blues and gospel, poetry with prose, and managing to critique the black experience of poverty while accepting support from a patron, Hughes was already modelling how he was as non-denominational in regards to genre as others such as James Joyce and Jackson Pollock.

Before graduating from Lincoln, where he was formally trained to be a teacher and not a writer, Hughes had two more memories to create. First, Hughes had a very distinguished role to play in the cultural event of the year when Countee Cullen married the daughter of W.E.B. Du Bois in April before 3,000 guests. Escorting the bride's mother down the aisle for all of Harlem to see, Hughes was 'embarrassed' to be wearing a 'hired suit that was faded' when Godmother would no doubt have bought him a new one.[35] What happened next became unforgettable to Hughes. Cullen, really in love with his best man Harold Jackman, set sail with Jackman and without the bride, leaving Hughes to paraphrase the *Afro-American* newspaper headline for decades to come: 'Groom Honeymoons with Best Man.'[36] Second, after confiding to Wallace Thurman that he was getting over his love interest in a woman named Laudee Williams, Hughes led a 24-page study on the state of a university educating black students.[37] Surveying nearly half the students, he was shocked to discover they voted 81–46 against having black faculty. The report went from a campus bulletin board straight to the front-page headline of the 6 April 1929 edition of the *Baltimore Afro-American* newspaper, stirring a conversation that reached all the way to Claude McKay in Europe. Langston had showed 'the courage of the innocent' that left him still beloved by the administration even as the faculty trembled.[38]

Graduating in June 1929, Hughes spent most of the summer rewriting *Not Without Laughter,* splitting time on his patron's dime between Pennsylvania, Baltimore and travels by train through Canada, starting in Montreal. Exhausted from revisions detailing how the blues are a sadness hardened by laughter, Mason sent him to Cuba charged with locating a composer for an opera she wanted him to write. Hughes simultaneously saw another welcome escape from the Depression's ever-deepening scars. He left the customs office in New York after a racist dispute where he was not allowed to buy tickets to Cuba. The dispute ended with frustration when Hughes defiantly enlisted the aid of the NAACP's Walter White. Eventually arriving in Havana, Hughes was disappointed when his recommended composer Amadeo Roldan 'squirmed before Langston's inquiries' and was not a suitable collaborator.[39] However, Hughes was introduced to Nicolás Guillén by José Antonio Fernández de Castro, spending a lovely evening at Lalita Zamora's restaurant in a group that also featured José's brother Jermandy as well as Gustavo Urrutia. Hughes was a star welcomed by all, and 'Lolita's', as he would write it in his notes, must have impressed, its owner being known nationally for her beauty.[40] In fact, after Hughes left, she sent letters praising his works, which she felt conveyed 'the sensation and feelings of the desires, hopes, loves, and ambitions of our race'.[41] This trip would eventually result in Hughes exerting remarkable influence throughout the Hispanic world. Often using his poems to reinforce local political goals, more than 164 of Hughes's poems have been translated throughout every Spanish-speaking country of the world, in more than three hundred different versions.[42]

Hughes famously left an indelible impression on the young Guillén when he very deliberately suggested that the poet incorporate Cuba's *son* tradition into his poems the way Hughes had done with America's sister musical form, the blues. Within days of his departure, Guillén composed eight poems in this vein so completely different from anything he had ever written that he was forever changed. The two men would remain in contact for decades, even as Guillén's leftist leanings eventually forced Cuba's National Poet into exile for five years before he returned in the early 1960s. It is in part because of this relationship that Hughes is still regarded as one of the most important poets in 'many parts of the Hispanic world, including Spain'.[43]

With the country's Mardi Gras celebration conveniently overlapping with his visit, Hughes's travelling companion Zell Ingram 'outdanced the natives', even teaching them an invented move he called the 'snakehips'.[44] Hughes travelled to the southern coastal town of Batabano to draft a poem titled after the city itself:

The children of this sea
are familiars of the sun.
They know its strange / caprichus [sic]
when the burning day is done.
They know its pale white lips
Ere the morning is begun.[45]

More interesting, Hughes drafted another unpublished poem during this trip. If the speaker was himself, as the tone seems to read, who was the 'you' in this intimate remembrance? We read, written in Hughes's hand:

Momento Habanero
Havana Hour

I touch your hand –
And then I go.
I kiss your lips –
And then I go.

You will forget,
I will forget,
And only time will know
You touched my hand,
I kissed your lips –
How swift sweet moments go.[46]

If Hughes was thinking of a play on words with 'Momento', was he thinking of 'Memento'? Eleven years later, Hughes would pen another unpublished work in which he noted 'send to Guillén':

A million miles of
nothing
Separates me from you.
You think it's something?
I do, too.[47]

One strains trying to surmise if the 'you' here is possibly Guillén, de Castro, Lalita herself, or some unnamed person Hughes met either during Mardi Gras or the group's nightly forays into Havana's Marianao district. As such, even this hidden poem reminds us of Hughes's steadfast devotion to the unknowability surrounding his sexuality. Not even his vast collection of unpublished work indexes anything more than his stubborn resistance to categories, and we cannot risk 'reinforcing a dangerous consensus of knowingness about the genuinely *un*known'.[48] Even with the full access we have, we also cannot expect his literary archive to ever reveal what Hughes carefully hid. Hughes consistently rejected the various markers for parsing sexual preference. Epistemologically, Hughes's unknowability mirrors the chameleon nature of every artist who shifts their persona from work to work.

Though often sensationalized when cast in films such as *Brother to Brother* (2004) and *Marshall* (2017), most thorough scholarship reveals the careful distinction that Hughes was intentionally (and forever) silent on this subject and thus 'sexually ambiguous'.[49] When he wrote in a very personal voice in 'Poem' (1925) that 'I loved my friend./ He went away from me', the dedication was merely to 'F.S.' Hughes – never named Ferdinand Smith, the Jamaican-born merchant seaman who had first 'influenced the poet to go to sea'.[50] The more interesting consideration is, why was Hughes so guarded about his sexuality? Some have wondered if he perhaps felt a burden as the unofficial Poet Laureate of his race, a position that might encourage him to conceal his homoerotic feelings. He may also have shunned the idea of being feminized.[51] Later, in the 1950s, legal enforcement against homosexual behaviour curbed people from admitting to something that was punishable by law. In the mid-1960s, as Carl Bean recalls, Hughes was sometimes more suggestive than before.[52] Most noteworthy is the way other New Negro-era performers also 'deferred a fixed subjectivity'.[53] In fact, 'unknowability' is a position, and Hughes was famous for guarding his privacy. Ada 'Bricktop' Smith asserted that she kept her 'private life private', and Josephine Baker likewise never addressed the subject. Ethel Waters married three times but also had lesbian lovers, as did Alberta Hunter.[54] Hughes was ever true to his Harlem sensibilities, all the way until his death when he wrote out the details for his 1920s-style funeral. Hughes resembled Lena Horne in 'refusing to corroborate' with the hegemony of labelling, thus keeping his sexual image always just out of reach.[55] In many ways, the not knowing can heighten erotic appeal by raising curiosity about a person precisely because they thwart classification.[56]

After three-and-a-half years with Godmother as his patron, Hughes was pushed away from Charlotte Mason's care in May 1930. No one has ever fully agreed on a single reason for their split, but Yuval Taylor believes Hughes was inadvertently getting in the way of Hurston completing her folklore project *Mules and Men* (1935), and Mason's 'last hope' of successful patronage among her African

Long before their relationship ended, Hughes joined Jessie Fauset (left) and
Zora Neale Hurston (right) on a tour through Tuskegee, Alabama, where they
visited Booker T. Washington's statue in 1927.

American protégés rested solely on 'Zora's unfinished manuscript'.[57]
There is no doubt Mason was suspicious of those she helped, old
enough to never be satisfied with even excessive gratitude, and
always expecting bigger results from her children's projects.
However, it seems most likely that Zora Neale Hurston forced a
wedge between the two by suggesting that Godmother's assistant,

Louise Thompson, and Hughes were misbehaving. Thompson, briefly the wife of Wallace Thurman in 1928, would become a sincere and close friend of Hughes for decades to come. A gifted public speaker, she invoked Hughes's poetry from the podium throughout her career.[58] She was also dismissed by Mason before Hughes's break, adding evidence to Hurston's interloping. With nothing tawdry going on, Hughes was absolutely broken by the fissure that, likely aimed at Thompson out of Hurston's jealousy, had inadvertently caught the poet with its shrapnel. Though less than a year after the stock market crash of Black Thursday, the withholding of financial assistance was not nearly so wrenching to Hughes as the emotional damage of not understanding Mason's separation. Poverty-stricken yet again, and in the worst era for it to happen, Hughes expressed his honest confusion to Mason in person (and through numerous letters) without even receiving the satisfaction of a reason. In the end, he could eventually only equate the split with the two other most disturbing events of his life. Only his father's anger and failure to see Jesus were on a par with this episode.[59]

With life resembling art, just before his split with Godmother, Zora Neale Hurston and Langston Hughes started collaborating on a play based on a folktale known as 'The Bone of Contention'. Hurston, who invited Hughes as her partner working '50–50', and even wrote she was willing 'to be 40 to your 60', had found the oral story during the early stages of the cultural anthropology work that would later make her famous.[60] The folk comedy centred around an incident where a mule bone is put to violent use to end a dispute between two hunters feuding about who shot a turkey. With Hughes and Hurston combining ideas of plot, dialogue and folk humour, Louise Thompson joined the couple as they created, typing drafts in April 1930.[61] Nearly finished with a first draft, Hurston halted the project and then headed back to the South and her folklore project.

Seven months later, with Thompson also having been dismissed by Godmother, Hurston copyrighted the play in her name as *De Turkey and de Law* on 28 October and sent it to Van Vechten without mentioning Hughes's involvement.[62] In a truly remarkable turn of events, the play started its production at the playhouse of Hughes's friends in the very city of Cleveland where Hughes was at the time visiting his mother Carrie. Hearing about the play for the first time in months, Hughes's shock was only elevated by the ensuing deception on the part of Hurston.

First, Zora confirmed to the production company on 17 January 1931 that the project is indeed a joint collaboration. The next day she also confessed Hughes's involvement to Van Vechten in an absolute 'tantrum', all the while assuring Godmother that the play was completely hers.[63] Having most likely already made her false claim about their non-existent romance, 'it became essential to Hurston to discredit both Hughes and Louise Thompson' to the woman who was still her own patron.[64] According to Yuval Taylor, Hughes's own mother wanted him to marry Louise, and 'One could easily make the case that she [Zora] was in love with him.'[65] Locke, under the same support as Hurston, 'bartered his soul' to maintain loyalty to Mason against an innocent (but now angry) Hughes.[66] Three days later, 20 January, brought a compromise, in which Hughes would accept one-third of the royalties. With the Gilpin Payers (the troupe set to stage the production) frustrated by all this confusion, they cancelled the play before it premiered in Cleveland.

Everything came to a head as 3 February brought Hurston to visit a bed-ridden Hughes, ill with both the flu and tonsillitis. With the play cancelled, and Louise herself in town, the remarkably athletic Zora fumed as she 'shook manuscripts' in Hughes's face. According to Hughes, she was claiming with each bicep that she wrote them all alone while 'Louise and I were off doing Spanish together. And the way she said *Spanish* meant something else.'[67] Though she would later claim false victory in a telegram sent swiftly to Godmother,

Hurston's visit actually ended when Hughes's mother screamed Zora straight out of the house in no uncertain terms. In fact it was so heated, Hughes wrote, 'I had to get up out of bed and restrain my mother.'[68] Such accusations of dishonesty, surely also believed by Charlotte Mason herself, left Hughes more than exhausted as he revealed that 'Violent anger makes me physically ill.'[69] Years later, Hurston would confess to Hughes's best friend, Arna Bontemps, 'the cross of her life is the fact that there has been a gulf between you and her . . . she wakes up at night crying about it even yet.'[70] When *Not Without Laughter* won the Harmon Foundation Award's prize of $400, the largest sum he had ever received, Hughes sent the award itself to Mason 'like a child' still wanting 'her admiration'.[71] In many ways the novel was hers, yet like his relationships with Hurston and Locke, Hughes's patronage under Godmother was over despite his final kindness.

4

In the USSR, 1930–33

Langston Hughes earned his radical reputation during the 1930s. Being revolutionary was not a phase Hughes merely passed through, and his earliest works also held these features. To help make this longer trajectory clear, one of the first landmark publications of Hughes's scattered works came when Hughes scholar and eventual biographer Faith Berry collected Hughes's writings on the topic under the title *Good Morning Revolution* in 1973. Hughes's volatile poetic statements, socialist stance on political issues and leftist professional memberships would result in false accusations for the rest of his life that he had formally joined the Communist Party. However, the fact that he never officially joined the party did not keep Hughes from mirroring its values, assisting in their causes and critiquing American capitalism throughout his career.

Hughes consistently attacked the economic structure dividing America's poorest citizens from its wealthiest. Imagining a corporate system that would soon sink to the very depths of the ocean, he wrote an unpublished poem simply titled 'Capitalism':

Ship
Going Nowhere
Old Wreckage
The Sea
Has not yet

Swallowed –
But will swallow.[1]

He was far more graphic in other verses from this era. In 'Revolution'
(1935), the mob is not out to claim a black lynch victim, but instead
to 'slaughter a capitalist "pig" that has been strung up and ready to
have his "golden throat" slit from "ear to ear"'.[2] Poems such as 'Wait'
(1933) also capture the voices of unrepentant workers of the world
who will speak with their hands even while they are on the verge of
being illiterate: 'I, silently,/ And without a single learned word/
Shall begin the slaughter.'[3]

One of the reasons for the escalation of Hughes's ire with his
homeland came as a result of the Scottsboro Case. Travelling by train
to their destination of Lookout Mountain, Tennessee, on 25 March
1931, nine black youths were falsely accused of raping two white
women in Scottsboro, Alabama. The case became an international
cause célèbre, and the International Labor Defense (ILD) took up the
case to defend the innocent while other organizations such as the
NAACP stood aside. The ILD's alignment with the Communist Party
USA would elevate both organizations to new heights throughout
the African American community as they fought to free the youths
who were nearly lynched before any trails could begin. Eight of the
defendants were originally sentenced to death. In the end none were
executed, but each spent between six-and-a-half and seventeen years
behind bars. One of the female accusers eventually stated plainly
that this punishment was undeserved: 'those policeman made me
tell a lie . . . those Negros did not touch me.'[4]

Hughes responded to the Scottsboro Case in measurable ways. In
doing so, he was not merely standing up for social justice. With the
defence team itself part of the fabric, Hughes was simultaneously
wrapped up with the left. To communicate that the issue was
straight from newspaper headlines, Hughes began his poem
'Scottsboro' (1931) with a large initial '8' that took up two full lines

leading into the words: 'BLACK BOYS IN A SOUTHERN JAIL./ WORLD, TURN PALE!'[5] Hughes's most potent response came when he was approached to submit something about the case to a little press in Chapel Hill, North Carolina. *Contempo*'s editor, Milton Abernathy, received a rushed letter from Hughes. Typed 22 October 1931, Hughes annotated his missive with as much, if not more, handwritten ink before redating it 23 October. Hughes apologized at the top by writing 'Pardon this ungodly letter', allowing some of his typed words to remain as he explained that in addition to the previous article he sent to be published in *Contempo*, 'Today I am enclosing two drawings by Zell Ingram . . . also a poem of mine which might be suitable for your Scottsboro issue.'[6] Communicating by hand that he is rushed for time, Hughes promises to alert them later of the date he will arrive in Chapel Hill. While Hughes's article was powerful, the poem 'Christ in Alabama' (1931) was a bombshell as Hughes openly compared the defendants in the case to Christ being crucified. The editors raised the stakes: given Hughes's open communication about when he would arrive, they withheld the 5,000 copies they had published with Hughes's poem and Ingram's image on the front until Hughes himself appeared in person. Having his appearance at the university initially banned, then finally relocated from the largest hall on Chapel Hill's campus to the smaller Gerrard Hall, Hughes appeared in person on 19 November while police stood guard outside the door. Smiling and telling light jokes, he diffused the tension and wisely passed on reading 'Christ in Alabama' aloud that evening.[7]

In the poem, Hughes flipped the myth of the South that led to so many black men being lynched. Rather than black men pursuing white women, Hughes reminded readers that the real history of the South featured white plantation owners taking black mistresses. Hughes reminded his readers that the 'White Master' had too often turned the 'Mammy of the South' into a mother. With that turn, Hughes suggested a possible psychological reason for lynching

Langston Hughes with a *Contempo* editor, Anthony Buttitta, on Franklin Street in Chapel Hill, North Carolina, with a still-standing church symbolically framed in the background to highlight the religious hypocrisy noted in 'Christ in Alabama' (November 1931).

itself, as white men can be understood to be externalizing a fear in response to a desire they know to be latent within themselves. The poem was so controversial that *Contempo* immediately saw all but one of its sponsors remove advertisements from its forthcoming issues. Editorials called for the governor himself to look into the matter and as far away as Charlotte one man wanted Hughes to be covered in a 'coat of tar'.[8]

After attending a party thrown by dramatist Paul Green that evening, Hughes skipped an expected appearance early the next morning and left town without receiving payment. When his cheque for $32.50 arrived in the post, he gladly consented to provide autographed poems to those who had dared support bringing such a controversial speaker to campus.[9] Hughes was later told that he was the first black man to eat at a restaurant on the still-famous Franklin Street where 'Nothing happened' as a result.[10] He had his photo taken with a church steeple that still stands today in the background, as if to connect his image of the black Christ with the religious hypocrisy he wrote of in the South.[11]

When Hughes arrived in Huntsville, Alabama, in early January 1932, he took the opportunity to send a one-cent postcard back to the *Contempo* editors. He wrote: 'Please send me copies of your last two numbers at Bethune-Cookman College, Datona, [*sic*] Florida, where I shall be till 9 January. People everywhere, to whom I show the paper are very much interested and want to know all about it.' And, perhaps in reference to both the near-lynching of the prisoners and the threats sent to him, Hughes also enclosed a copy of 'The Town of Scottsboro'. In this poem he extended what the headlines read in his earlier poem 'Scottsboro' by adding the personal investigation reminiscent of a correspondent. He could now declare with the authority of personal reporting about this town: 'No shame is writ across its face –/ Its court, too weak to stand against a mob,/ Its people's heart, too small to hold a sob.'[12] The bottom of the poem reads 'At Scottsboro, January 2, 1932', and in black ink Hughes wrote

Dear Contempo—raries —
Why don't you set up here
and get tarred and feathered —

THE TOWN OF SCOTTSBORO

Scottsboro's just a little place:
No shame is writ across its face---
Its court, too weak to stand against a mob,
Its people's heart, too small to hold a sob.

Langston Hughes

At Scottsboro,
January 2, 1932

Original version of 'The Town of Scottsboro' sent to *Contempo* editors from Scottsboro, Alabama, on 2 January 1932. Hughes had earlier tried to meet in person with one of the accusers and heard rumours that he might be lynched.

across the top: 'Dear Contempo-raries— Why don't you set up here and get tarred and feathered—.'[13] Hughes had arrived in Huntsville, where he visited the despondent prisoners. He was repeatedly dissuaded from meeting with one of the women who had made false accusations of rape, and he received letters from friends worrying that he would 'surely be lynched'.[14]

Hughes's reading tour through the South had been the idea of Mary McCloud Bethune, who told him 'people need poetry', and his arrival in January at the college that bore her name proved she was right.[15] Unable ever to drive himself, Hughes had secured W. Radcliffe Lucas to be his driver. Hughes spent over $600 of the $1,000 Rosewald Fund he had been awarded for the trip on a new Model A Ford Sedan, posters, portraits, postage and the purchase of his own books to sell at each stop.[16] Judging by one photograph, Hughes evidently used all his money on these supplies, as he can be seen wearing oversized trousers as he stands next to Lucas. To try and amend this, Hughes often accepted as much as $50 for an appearance – or as little as nothing, depending on the particulars – and by the end he had completed 54 readings with a net profit of $1,337.83. Along the way he gladly shared the stage with Father of the Blues W. C. Handy and met inventor George Washington Carver. He always invested in the younger generation of writers and upon meeting the future luminary Margaret Walker she would remember how Hughes cared so much that he 'stopped what he was doing . . . and went through my poems one by one for about an hour'.[17] This practice was to have a lasting impact; in another generation, the unrelated Alice Walker, another renowned writer he would encourage, would do 'more than most to carry on Langston's legacy and spirit'.[18]

After the tour, Hughes would note his deep anger at the docility he witnessed from so many black colleges who never spoke of current issues such as the Scottsboro Case. He wrote publically in 'Cowards from the Colleges' (1934) that the race had better 'look to the unlettered for their leaders, and expect only cowards from the

colleges'.[19] Hughes collected his poems about Scottsboro alongside
a play he had written, and published them under the title *Scottsboro
Limited* (1932). With proceeds from the book going to the Scottsboro
Defense Fund, the cover image itself used nine telegraph wires to
suggest the legal lynching of each of the figures it portrayed.[20]
Nothing sold better on this tour than Hughes's one-dollar pamphlet
of poems entitled *The Negro Mother*. In Birmingham, Alabama, they
sold 'like reefers on 131st street' in New York.[21] The title poem had
been inspired by Bethune herself, and a packed hall heard Hughes
read it in her presence after a hundred-person choir performed.
The highlight of the tour came when Bethune cried 'My son, my
son' with tears in her eyes as she rushed to the podium to hug
Hughes after he read the poem.[22]

During a tour stop at Oakwood Junior College in Alabama,
Hughes deepened his relationship with the man who would soon
become his closest lifelong friend. Arna Bontemps, who bore a
startlingly similar appearance to Hughes, was a prominent poet
himself, and Hughes would exchange more letters with Bontemps
than any other person over the course of his lifetime. Having taught
in Harlem, and authored both a novel and a play with Countee
Cullen, Bontemps was a happily married man who would end
up at Fisk University in Nashville in later years. Whenever the
youngest of the four Bontemps children needed to be photographed,
they always ended up in Hughes's arms, each one laughing more
naturally than with the happy parents themselves.

At this time the two collaborated on a book of children's
literature titled *Popo and Fifina* (1932). Inspired by Hughes's recent
visit to Haiti in early 1931, the novella also introduces what would
become Hughes's central theme of the dream. During a seemingly
innocent scene, Popo and Fifina play with 'a lovely delicate kite' that
'soar[s] in the clouds – like a wish or a dream'.[23] Their kite is called
'a big scarlet star rising' and 'a great red star', but in the midst of
the children's fun, a 'stranger's kite, a dull brown thing' reminds

Popo 'of a hawk swooping over a smaller bird'. The boy flying the hawk-kite purposely tries to take down Popo's red star by entangling it, 'but Popo had confidence in the kite Papa Jean had made him [and] believed his big red star-kite was a match for any hawk'.[24] Does Popo's red star-kite represent the 'dream' of communism facing a hawk-kite representative of the eagle of American capitalism? If so, this dream was linked to socialism, not America. Hughes would have been more than aware during his stay in Haiti that American forces had been occupying the country since 1915 with the goal of eliminating its communist ideologies. In the end, Popo's red star-kite is victorious: 'but the other one, the hawk, was falling to the earth like an evil bird with a broken wing'.[25]

Always one to overlap texts from one project to the next as he was composing, this image reappears in a poem from one of Hughes's most reprinted books, *The Dream Keeper*, first published the very same year in 1932. In lines that would inspire generations of readers, Hughes found that 'if dreams die/ Life is a broken-winged bird/ That cannot fly.'[26] Had Hughes turned the American dream into something that would fail in *Popo and Fifina*, or did he take this image of aspiration from 'Dreams' and later amend it into a critique of capitalism?

With each of these works, Hughes was continuing a tradition of writing for children that dated back to his very earliest publications when he placed twelve separate works in *The Brownies' Book* from January to November 1921. Hughes's class consciousness shines through in almost all of these pieces, revealing that the more vibrant works of the 1930s must be read as extensions of his earliest feelings. In one example from 1921, Hughes's *Those Who Have No Turkey*, a boy and girl slip a golden coin into an old woman's pouch to demonstrate the act of sharing equally. Having eschewed the joys of monetizing, Rosa says: 'I'm happier than any wooden clock could make me.' Hughes ends the play by describing the couple sitting in front of their fireplace, which gives off a 'warm red light'.[27] Even if this light isn't red to indicate communist leanings, Hughes's subject-matter seeks to train the next generation in spreading wealth instead of amassing capital.

Louise Thompson's friendship with Hughes continued even after both had been dismissed by Godmother. In fact, Louise continued collaborating with Hughes and personally typed one of Hughes's most sarcastic poems, 'Advertisement for the Waldorf Astoria', before it was sent to Whittaker Chambers for publication.[28] Published in *New Masses* in December 1931, the poem was inspired by an advertisement Hughes saw in *Vanity Fair* for the new $28-million hotel he walked by regularly during the Depression.[29] As he would write to Carl Van Vechten, he was deeply angered and had to risk 'the shame of the future' for the 'impulse of the moment' after seeing the poor nearby in lines so long they 'couldn't reach the soup kitchens'.[30] He paired these hungry and homeless workers he saw all around New York City with those who lived on caviar and dressed in furs. Accompanied with full illustrations by Walter Steinhilber that anticipate images used in today's graphic novels, viewers saw the rich arriving in limousines driven across roads where starving workers huddled underground. Hughes railed against the rich: 'a thousand nigger section-hands keep the roadbeds smooth,/ so investments in railroads pay ladies with diamond/ necklaces staring at Cert [*sic*] murals'.[31] The reference to Sert, a Spanish painter whose work *American Progress* (1937) would soon replace the famously controversial mural by Diego Rivera in Rockefeller Center, is a reminder that the hotel had its own large mural by Sert hanging in a room named after him. Apparently neither Langston nor Louise caught the misspelling of José María Sert's name that has been corrected in later reprintings.

What Hughes did catch, thanks to Louise, was the *Europa* as it left port on 14 June taking Hughes to the USSR in 1932. Hughes received a telegram from Thompson on 9 May to be part of a 22-person cast to make a Russian film based on American racism

At her invitation, Langston joined Louise Thompson and another twenty African Americans as they set sail on the *Europa* in June 1932 to make a film in the USSR that never materialized.

titled *Black and White*. He was the very last passenger to board that day, 'staggering under the weight of his bags, his typewriter, a Victrola, and a box of blues and jazz records'.[32] Passing through Berlin before arriving in Leningrad by train, Hughes would find himself at the centre of a small band that came to be named the 'L-raising Trio', as Langston, Loren Miller and Louise Thompson soon found themselves sharing most meals together. (Miller was a young black communist lawyer who had supported Hughes's work by unsuccessfully trying to get one of his controversial plays staged in Los Angeles.) The larger group, as Hughes explained, consisted of 'an art student just out of Hampton, a teacher, a female elocutionist from Seattle, three would-be writers other than myself, a very pretty divorcée who traveled on alimony, a female swimming instructor, and various clerks and stenographers'.[33] In sum, only two members of the group were professional performers, each having played only minor roles on stage before.[34] When they all posed for a group photo, Hughes threw a white coat over his collarless shirt. Desperate for money during the Depression, each jumped at the all-expenses-paid trip. Given 400 rubles a month and full accommodation, the group was paraded about and 'invited to receptions, museums, factories', appearing regularly in 'front-page photographs and news stories'.[35]

While the Russian Comintern, the very centre of decision making in the USSR, hoped to show the racial divide that existed in America as counter-propaganda to its own state of race relations, key weaknesses in the planning immediately emerged. The script had been written by a Russian with no knowledge of the film's setting in Birmingham, Alabama. Moreover, the cast themselves were expected to sing, but none could carry a tune except for Sylvia Garner. Even with such challenges, Hughes was charged to revise the script when suddenly the film was halted for reasons the group would never fully understand. In a complex game where propaganda and progress collided, American engineer Colonel Hugh L. Cooper learned of the movie's goals and feared that the fallout of portraying American racism on screen would forever shape Russian attitudes about the USA. The matter reached Stalin himself, who had placed Cooper in charge of a dam that would serve as the new country's largest symbol of industrial expertise. When Cooper threatened to stop building the Dnieprostroi Dam if *Black and White* went forward, Stalin consented to drop the film. He tried to avoid full humiliation by announcing filming would be postponed until the following year.[36]

Though Paris papers would soon accurately suggest that the film was never going to be made, the Soviet Trade Union stepped in to offer the crew a tour of the USSR that extended as far as Turkmenistan. With a group of seven others Hughes gladly accepted going where outsiders were rarely allowed to travel, keen to see how socialism dealt with issues of poverty and race.[37] Hughes was soon making more money from individual publications in Russia than he had made collectively over the course of his entire career in America. Along with his novel *Not Without Laughter* being translated into Russian, he accepted 2,000 rubles to write six to ten articles for a Russian newspaper, and another 60,000 for a translation into Uzbek of *The Weary Blues*.[38] Tragically, poet Sanjar Siddiq, the man who translated Hughes's poetry into Uzbek as he travelled with Hughes, was later executed in one of Stalin's many purges in 1938.[39]

Red letters paid better than black words, and Hughes set to writing with more energy than he had ever spent before, growing confident he could make a real living as a writer. Feeling as free of race as others such as Claude McKay and Paul Robeson had before him, Hughes explained:

I have noticed a definite lack of hatred against me as a black man . . . In France or Italy, racism is supposedly nonexistent, but when I was in those countries a few years ago, I felt that I was merely tolerated. I never felt as I did today, that my skin color was unimportant.[40]

With Dorothy West on the *Europa*, 1932. She declared she wanted to have Langston's child and then leave him alone to wander the world.

He also eschewed poetic ambiguity in favour of philosophical declarations. In the poem 'Good Morning Revolution' (1932), Hughes altered Carl Sandburg's own *Good Morning, America* (1928) to declare uprising and revolution were going to take 'All the tools of production' and 'turn 'em over to the people who work./ Rule and run 'em for us people who work.'[41] Rhyme, cadence and musicality were replaced by manifestos and exclamation points. The proletariat was on the march, and it would not stop until even America was changed. In 'One More "S" in the USA' (1934), Hughes pleaded that his own countrymen could change the USA to make it mirror the USSR: 'Come together, fellow workers/ Black and White can all be red' as the bankers of the world were all organizing 'For another great big war.'[42]

Hughes continued writing. The fifty-page pamphlet *A Negro Looks at Soviet Central Asia* (1934) was penned while he unexpectedly met a younger Hungarian journalist who was working for a Berlin newspaper. Arthur Koestler, who would later be known as a writer of distinction, seemed unimpressed by what he observed of Russia, while Hughes was energized. It was Koestler who encouraged Hughes to write about what he saw in the union meetings, mills and factories in Ashkhabad.[43] Several of these pieces would appear in various places over time, and a promising new project is currently under way to map the exact GPS coordinates of Hughes's trip, to evaluate the long-term status of many of the people and topics he described.[44]

Deeply impressed by the parade of workers rather than the planes and tanks that were passing what seemed to be a 'million people', Hughes was less than 100 yards away from Stalin himself on May Day 1933.[45] But during his time in Russia there were several famous women Hughes saw from an even closer proximity. Dorothy West, one of the cast members of the defunct film, proposed marriage, letting him know she wanted to have his child before leaving the poet free to wander the wide world without her.[46] In addition, a Russian actress Hughes would refer to only as 'Natasha' had become so enamoured with him that she left her husband

and gathered all her savings to unexpectedly board Hughes's Trans-Siberian Express. She was intending to travel with him across the country (and beyond) but was let down and sent away from her reluctant new lover at the first rail stop.[47] Instead of this surprise, Hughes was expecting a heartfelt goodbye from her such as the one he received a year earlier with Anna, another woman with whom he had shared similar intimacies earlier in Haiti. On that occasion, she and Coloma, Zell Ingram's lover, watched 'weeping on the shore' as the two men sailed away.[48]

In addition to these women, Sylvia Chen seemed to capture Hughes's heart and imagination in a relationship that was as serious as any the poet could ever claim. Sylvia (or Si-lan) was a remarkable dancer who combined Chinese and Western choreography into her performances. She found herself in Moscow because of her own radical politics, having been raised in both Trinidad and England. Hughes had frequented her company day and night at the Metropole Hotel, with Chen later acknowledging that 'Langston was the first man I was ever intimate with.'[49] Chen often dressed in 'tight, high-necked Chinese dresses with a slit in the side'. Hughes left her elegance behind, neither definitively accepting nor rejecting what it seems were discussions of marriage.[50] Soon they were trading poems, with Chen sending a parody of Robert Burns's 'A Red, Red Rose' (1794); she ended: 'And do I love you? Dear, I think so deep in love am I/ That I would come to you my dear, though t'were/ Ten thousand miles.'[51] With his time in Moscow ended, and probably never having seen her dance, Hughes was noncommittal in his personal encounters and now proceeded to express himself playfully in a long-distance romance where he would write: 'I want you, Sylvia baby, more than anyone else in the world, believe it or not. I love you . . . Wish I could kiss you! Do You?'[52] Four months later Hughes was again writing: 'Who wants to *talk* anyhow. Will you kiss me next time or not? Heh? You better! What nationality would our baby be anyhow?'[53]

Hughes toured the interior of the USSR while getting to know the young Arthur Koestler. Here Hughes dons a Beluchi turban near Merv, Turkmenistan, in 1932.

Eventually, Hughes turned his energy for writing love letters towards his creative projects, and a full year before he learned it, Chen had married. Either frustrated with his own indecision and lack of financial standing or just regretting losing her, he fired off a letter filled with such rage at her for not waiting to marry him that Chen destroyed it immediately.[54] When the two would finally meet again years later, Hughes spoke with tears in his voice: 'Why did you do it!? How could you give up what we had and marry someone else when I met you first?'[55] Hughes would only consider marriage one other time, but that decision never moved him to this emotional level.

As Hughes continued the 8,851-kilometre (5,500-mi.) train ride across Russia's Ural Mountains without 'Natasha', West or Chen, he was approaching the far eastern reaches of the continent on his way back to America, via Japan. Re-wearing the same grey trousers that had once been white, he boldly wrapped a Beluchi turban around his head and posed for a photograph in Turkmenistan. The country he left behind was 'the only place I've ever made enough to live from writing'.[56] As he would later write, 'I wish I could commute between Harlem and the Metropol [hotel in Moscow].'[57] Moreover, where in America would he ever get such medical treatment? When he was ill, word reached the government that an important guest needed help, and Hughes was treated without charge by the president of Uzbekistan's personal physician.[58] It is no wonder that as far as he would indeed wander, Hughes held Russia and its socialist practices in the highest regard for years to come.

His extended stay in Russia raised the international community's suspicions about Hughes's political activities. Losing some much-desired anonymity when he stayed at Frank Lloyd Wright's Imperial Hotel in Tokyo, news photographers and leading officials soon discovered his whereabouts and arranged for interviews. Hughes failed to realize he was under surveillance until it was too late. He was detained for six hours while serious questions were cast upon his behaviour, requiring him to make official statements (that were then altered by his inquisitors) about what he had been doing for more than a year in Russia.[59] Hughes was forced to leave the country immediately with the documents gathered in his dossier being passed to the U.S. State Department. After having his room and personal belongings searched in Japan, including every document he carried with him, Hughes was not greeted but rather 'met' by an FBI agent when he arrived in Honolulu, Hawaii.[60] This was only the beginning of the increased surveillance Hughes would be subjected to in the years ahead.

5

Let America Be America Again, 1933–40

Back on the American continent for the first time in fourteen months, Hughes was greeted in California by driver Eddie Pharr, who then drove a cream-coloured limousine up to his white employer's mansion overlooking the San Francisco Bay. Such arrangements were made possible much earlier when, near the end of Hughes's gruelling book tour across the South in 1931, Noël Sullivan, a wealthy concert singer who also served as a patron to African American artists, had invited Hughes to enjoy an extended stay with him in California. Now Hughes was being quickly whisked away to Sullivan's cottage, Ennesfree, and soon the owner's separate residence in Carmel-by-the-Sea was set up for Hughes to write in privacy.[1] Langston Hughes would never look more handsome than in the photographs he brought back from his travels, looking up coyly as he held a Russian copy of *Not Without Laughter* or standing firmly in another photo featuring a Honolulu smile. It would be many years until his front teeth would need a bridge and still two years until he started grooming his signature moustache. Accompanied by Greta, Sullivan's German shepherd, Hughes continued the spirited task he had begun in Russia of writing short stories. Inspired by his reading of D. H. Lawrence's 'The Lovely Lady' (1932), Hughes had already placed two short stories in the prominent u.s. magazine *American Mercury*. Earning $100 each for these stories, Blanche Knopf, who had personally placed them in the H. L. Mencken publication herself, now turned over these

Hughes holding a Russian translation of his novel *Not Without Laughter*, Moscow, 1933. Hughes received larger payments for his work in Russia than he ever had in America.

duties to Maxim Lieber, the man who would serve as Hughes's literary agent for years to come.[2]

Sullivan's wealth, political consciousness, white skin and racial ease made accepting the arrangement as easy for Hughes as it had been for previous visitors such as Roland Hayes, Marian Anderson and Duke Ellington. Sullivan's patronage of the arts, Paris education in singing and involvement with the left had allowed the Roman Catholic to invest his resources in many noble causes, including the local John Reed Club, where Hughes was soon to appear.[3] With Hughes writing one short story a week, Lieber, who also represented the likes of Richard Wright and Thomas Wolfe, soon placed 'Home' (1934) and 'Slave on the Block' (1933) in *Esquire* and *Scribner's*.[4] The short-story form had actually been among Hughes's first forays into writing since placing three short stories in his high school paper's *Monthly* magazine.[5]

By December 1933 Hughes had twelve stories collected under the title *The Ways of White Folks*. Having spent a full year living rent-free

Returning to the U.S. after fourteen months away, Hughes smiles here despite being met by FBI agents who learned of his interrogation in Japan, 1933.

On the California beach near Carmel-by-the-Sea, Hughes was free to write short stories and enjoy time with Noël Sullivan's dog Greta, 1933.

at his home, Hughes aptly dedicated the book to Sullivan himself. Hughes's stories depict miscegenation in 'Red-headed Baby' (1934), where the white Clarence comes back to the black Betsy only to discover that his last visit had resulted in the conception of their child. Thinking of an imagined fate for an actual musician such as Louis Jones, Hughes created black violinist Roy Williams, who returns to Missouri in 'Home' to be dragged, stripped naked and lynched simply for speaking publicly to the white Miss Reece.[6] The image of 'the Aeolian harp is resignified by Hughes as Roy's body swings "like a violin for the wind to play."'[7] Playing off the title of W.E.B. Du Bois' *The Souls of Black Folks* (1903), Hughes's stories revealed as much about white behaviour as they did about black interiority. As such, the 'opening description of Dora Ellsworth was actually Godmother Charlotte Mason in "The Blues I'm Playing".'[8] The collection earned praise, hailed as his 'strongest work to date' by *Saturday Review* and 'some of the best short stories that have appeared in this country in years' by *North American Review*.[9]

While most arrived there to seek a quick divorce under the state's forgiving legal statutes, Hughes instead disappeared for eight weeks to Reno, Nevada, to continue writing in a place where only three people knew his address.[10] Carmel became uninhabitable when the California iteration of the KKK, known as the Vigilantes, brought Hughes into the sights of its supremacist views and race hatred. The Vigilantes knocked on doors at night to terrorize those they singled out, such as muck-raking journalist Lincoln Steffens. Hughes left Carmel in a way that then-resident and poet Robinson Jeffers or the former Robert Louis Stevenson, author of the *Strange Case of Dr Jekyll and Mr Hyde* (1886), would never have to imagine. Hughes feared for his life after consecutive verbal attacks were made against him in the local newspaper amid nights of ever-closer door-to-door harassments. One of these stories asserted: 'White girls have ridden down the street with him, smiling [into] his face . . . magazines have spread his communist doctrines to thousands and thousands of American Homes. Russia would be a good place for Hughes.'[11]

In Reno, while writing the unpublished story 'Mailbox for the Dead', Hughes experienced what he called a 'psychic' experience as his father died while he was thinking about him.[12] Some biographers have been less convinced, rightly noting that Hughes had known of his father's illness weeks before.[13] However, Hughes needed to continue writing. In fact, while in Reno for eight weeks before this event, Hughes had become so desperate for funds that he hatched a plan to publish three stories from Reno under the pseudonym 'David Boatman'. The plan failed when the stories were sent by his editor with attributions to Hughes himself. None would be accepted for publication if they did not include racial subject-matter, and as a result, Hughes borrowed funds from his uncle John S. P. Hughes to make the long train ride from Los Angeles to Mexico City, quietly hopeful that his father's estate might yield a much-needed boost to the finances of his only child. Hughes arrived later than expected after being detained for two days near the Arizona border for the humiliating experience of American officials demanding he be cleared for a permit that needed to state he was 'colored'. In a telenovela-type experience, when the will was read aloud, Hughes's name was nowhere to be found. Not even his father's new wife had received a peso as James Hughes left everything to the Patiño sisters – Lola, Fela and Cuca – who had cared for most of his daily needs and loyally made arrangements for his funeral. Though he was not listed in the will, the sisters nonetheless insisted that Hughes divide with them what was left of his father's now depleted estate.[14]

Staying on at the Patiño sisters' insistence, Hughes remained in Mexico City for six months, where he walked past Diego Rivera frescos almost every day.[15] Hughes met the famous muralist, but would go on to spend more pages writing about Lupe Marín in his second autobiography than he devoted to the more famous Frida Kahlo, to whom Rivera was then married.[16] With formal proceedings held up when his father's widow sued unsuccessfully, Hughes finally received his share of the estate. In the end, the money in his father's bank account was split four ways, with the sisters retaining ownership of the ranch and other land holdings. Hughes barely had enough money to pay back his Uncle John and friends

Matt and 'Nebby' Crawford, and redeem the wristwatch he had pawned to pay for the trip.[17]

Hughes returned to New York for the first time in over three years, excited that his play *Mulatto* was set to open on Broadway for the 1935 season. Having just delivered the most important address of his life before a crowd of 4,000 at the University of Minnesota, and with many more listening on radio, Hughes unpacked his bags at Toy and Emerson Harper's home in Harlem before attending the rehearsals, where Rose McClendon was starring in the lead role.[18] However, his excitement was short-lived when he curiously heard actors 'reading lines I'd never written'.[19] The play was funded and produced by Martin Jones, who had made a small fortune on a sensational play, *White Cargo* (1923). Now Jones was intent on another commercial hit, separating Hughes from his royalties and adding his own name as author.[20]

If Hughes ever thought that this might be his way of getting the last laugh with Zora Neale Hurston over *Mule Bone*, he needed only the humiliation of opening night to remind him of the cut-throat business of the theatre. Jones planned an after party where no black people – including Hughes himself – were invited. When Hughes learned that blacks were being steered away from premier seating for the performance as well, he promptly bought as many tickets as he could afford and gave them all away to the darkest friends he knew (including Claude McKay). Hughes skipped the premiere of his own opening, later lamenting that he wished the show would close rather than leave him to 'sit here penniless to the point of notoriety'.[21] Despite the most damaging reviews of Hughes's life, it would not close, running for a full year then travelling for another two seasons.[22] Hughes spent endless hours and energy fighting for royalties and promised advances only to be consistently shortchanged by the belligerent Jones.

In its bastardized form, *Mulatto* eventually earned Hughes distinction as the longest running play on Broadway ever written by an African American. As years would pass, it would seem an achievement when only *A Raisin in the Sun* had surpassed its run – 25 years later in 1959. Hughes had been writing about the figure of the tragic mulatto since he published the poem 'Cross' in 1925. Because it was such a volatile topic, Hughes read the poem loudly 'to awaken all sleepers' at his poetry readings, quickly learning that when it ended 'I knew I had the complete attention of my listeners again.'[23] The poem is based on an actual encounter Hughes had with a sixteen-year-old boy he met on his first voyage to Africa.[24] The speaker notes that his father died in the comfort of a big house, but 'My ma died in a shack./ I wonder where I'm gonna die,/ Being neither white nor black?'[25]

Now, in the play *Mulatto*, Hughes created Robert Lewis, the son of the white Colonel Tom and his mistress the black Cora. Wanting the same privileges afforded to the colonel, Robert ends up killing his father, and spending the rest of the play running from a lynch mob. Three decades later many noted the resemblance between Robert and the hero of James Baldwin's *Blues for Mister Charlie* (1964).[26] As 'no single genre even imprisoned Langston Hughes, who rebelled against formal limits as easily as he opposed social ones', Hughes also used this plot for his short story 'Father and Son' (1933).[27] One key twist is that Robert (now 'Bert') ends up shooting himself at the end. Following historical parallels, the mob lynches his dead body anyway so they can claim they killed him themselves. Hughes understood the dislocation between reality and the news. As such, he inserted a fictional news clipping at the end of the story that allowed 'the realms of literature and journalism to merge'.[28] 'Father and Son' eventually 'undermines the legitimacy of mainstream newspaper accounts because Hughes's fictional story is more real than the news itself'.[29] In poetry, prose or plays, Hughes explored a topic that was still very much outside of the mainstream in the 1930s. Hughes later revived this story in his opera *The Barrier* (1950), suggesting the investment he made to try to bring this subject out of the bedroom and onto the stage.

Where dreams had captured the hope and inspiration Hughes hoped to pass on to the young in his earlier writings, featured in *The Dream Keeper*, the dream then became a trope of critique as Hughes continued writing in the Great Depression. One of his most celebrated poems was written on a train ride from New York to visit his mother in Oberlin, Ohio. In 'Let America Be America Again', the dream serves as a means to highlight where America has faltered on its promises:

> Let America be America again.
> Let it be the dream it used to be.
> Let it be the pioneer on the plain
> Seeking a home where he himself is free.
> (America never was America to me.)[30]

Reminding readers that the country is still a hope that remains unachieved, the speaker longs for a nation that is not meant to *seem*, but *be*: 'Let America be the dream the dreamers dreamed.'[31] The speaker represents all the workers in the supposed land of the free. He is the slave, the poor, the indigenous, all who made America through sweat and pain. This plea slowly became a declaration that readers of the 1936 *Esquire* magazine were not permitted to read as the magazine chose to publish only the first fifty lines of Hughes's poem so that the work could fit on one page illustrated with artwork by Mitchell Siporin. Given the startling image of a lynching, Hughes accepted their choice, but wished that what he called the poem's 'dialectical solution' would have been included as well.[32] It also carried echoes of Woody Guthrie's 'This Land Is Your Land' (1940) as well as so many of Walt Whitman's verses that included invocations of classic American anthems. This poem, with others such as 'The Negro Mother', would be sung from stages starting in 1941.[33]

Though it would not be published for another five years, it was also during 1936 that Hughes penned his signature poem 'I Dream a World'. Again, the future is simultaneously a critique of the present as the speaker reminds listeners of what does not currently exist:

I dream a world where all
Will know sweet freedom's way
Where greed no longer saps the soul
Nor avarice blights our day.
A world I dream where black or white
Whatever race you be
Will share the bounties of the earth
And every man is free.[34]

Hughes elevated the final four lines above by having them placed inside personalized Christmas cards he sent in 1954 with a vibrant colour image of black and white children dancing hand in hand around a lit Christmas tree, drawn by Rockwell Kent.[35] The poem, eventually printed in over fifty different publications, was originally drafted and used as dialogue in his opera-in-progress, then called *Emperor of Haiti* (later *Troubled Island*).[36] Walled away from the world to write for eighteen consecutive days at the Majestic Hotel in Cleveland, Hughes might have thought of an image from his earlier poem 'Mister Sandman' (1921). In that poem, he wrote: 'I'll send a dream like a precious pearl.'[37] In 'I Dream a World', those who wake with 'joy, like a pearl' seem to figuratively have sand fall out of a closed eye that is shaped like a shell. Hughes's emphasis here is on sharing the material goods of the world so that prosperity is available to all. The very fact that this speaker has to hope for this in the future reveals its current absence in the world.

After speaking before 10,000 people in Cleveland attending the Third U.S. Congress against War and Fascism in early January 1936,

Hughes addressed the Second International Writers' Congress the next year in Paris. Part of his appeal on that day rests on what reads as an angrier prose rendition of 'I Dream a World', also framed by a similar repetition of anaphora:

> We Negros of America are tired of a world divided superficially on the basis of blood and color, but in reality on the basis of poverty and power – the rich over the poor, no matter what their color. We Negroes in America are tired of a world in which it is possible for any group of people to say to another: 'You have no right to happiness, or freedom, or the joy of life.' We are tired of a world where forever we work for someone else and the profits are not ours.[38]

The last word, 'ours', is another perfect echo to the final line of 'I Dream a World': 'Of such I dream our world.' 'Our' would continue to be the preferred collective pronoun for Hughes, and when he spoke at the Third American Writers' Congress in Carnegie Hall two years later, he would again emphasize that 'It is not a matter of *mine* and *yours*. It is a matter of *ours*.'[39]

'I Dream a World' resonated across the Cleveland stage as *Troubled Island* became the highlight of the city's theatrical season. The night it premiered, 18 November 1936, the musician Margaret Bonds introduced the poet to her friend, the 22-year-old Elsie Roxborough, who was, as playwright Arthur Miller described, 'the most striking girl in Ann Arbor'.[40] A student and performer of theatre at the University of Michigan, Roxborough's stunning beauty was further buoyed by her family success. A rich uncle was also her professional stage manager, and she was the daughter of Michigan's first black senator. Carrying herself with 'the assurance of someone born to beauty', she fell in love with Hughes, proposing marriage to him at least three times.[41] Hughes refused, citing both poverty born from writing poetry and probably fretting about both her age difference of twelve years as well as the racial shame she felt about her light skin.[42] She had just been linked as a possible lover to boxer Joe Louis before they met, but five months later every black newspaper in the u.s. carried another story: Hughes and Elsie were about to marry. Hughes refuted the story, then made his position unmistakably clear to her in person when he attended her own production of *Troubled Island*, now titled *Drums of Haiti*, in Detroit. However, she would be denied but never swayed as she continued to send amorous letters, one signed 'Elizabeth Barret Browning' and sent to her 'hoped-for Robert Browning'.[43]

She maintained her love for Hughes over the years, with more letters arriving and kept by Hughes. When she finally turned to passing as white under different aliases, and exchanging her 'raven hair' for blonde, the unhappy actress, model and writer overdosed in 1949 in what may well have been a suicide.[44] Hughes responded by moving her photograph from the Harper's downstairs piano up to his personal study, where he answered questions about her identity 'only in a guarded way'.[45] It is unclear when the couple officially parted ways as multiple friends were sure they spotted her arriving too late to bid Hughes goodbye as he sailed for Paris in July 1938.[46]

Cancelling a sixty-day tour through Russia that he was slated to lead, Hughes left to cover the Spanish Civil War on 30 June 1937.[47] The *Baltimore Afro-American* newspaper sent him abroad to write 'trench-coat prose' about black Americans volunteering in the International Brigades with articles being picked up by other news outlets such as Cleveland's *Call-post* and *Globe* magazine.[48] Hughes's 22 articles covered an angle no one else in the world was focused on as companies such as the Abraham Lincoln and Washington Brigades were not only integrated but featured Negro commanders leading white troops, 'a policy then unheard of in the u.s. Army'.[49] Overcoming outright denials by the u.s. State Department, Hughes

Ministerio de

El Jefe de la Oficina de Prensa

CERTIFICA que Langston Hughes figura inscrito
en el Registro de Periodistas Extranjeros de
esta Oficina, como corresponsal de "Globe Magazine", "Afro American" de Baltimore, y "Call-
Post" de Cleveland.
Valencia, 30 de Julio de 1937.

When the U.S. stalled in granting Hughes his press credentials to cover the Spanish
Civil War in 1937, he secured entry through French channels.

struggled to enter Spain in early August, finally securing press
credentials through French means.[50]

In lighter moments, Hughes stood among black soldiers such as
Thaddeus Battle and Bunny Rucker like a schoolboy hearing gossip
about a girl he just met. In fact, his laugh often sounded as if he was
being tickled. Staying for five months, housed mostly in the Alianza
overlooking Madrid, Hughes took on the imagined voice of one of
the international brigades' black soldiers in two poems written as
'Postcard from Spain' (1938) and 'Letter from Spain' (1937).[51]
Addressed to fictional family members back home in Alabama, the
poems are dated and signed 'Johnny'. The letter imagines befriending
a 'Moorish prisoner' who has been duped into fighting for Franco
while the postcard exults a new-found feeling of companionship as
'Folks over here don't treat me/ Like white folks used to do.'[52] Hughes
sent the nearly identical first draft of his 'Postcard' as a literal postcard
to Louise Thompson, writing it on the back of an image of Hans
Beimler, a German Communist Party member who was killed leading

Hughes standing with Mikhail Koltsov, Ernest Hemingway and Cuban poet Nicolás Guillén. Hemingway himself threw Hughes's farewell party when he left Madrid in 1937.

forces against Spanish Nationalists in 1936, before Hughes arrived. Though the subject-matter was serious, his sense of humour could not be contained as he playfully signed off 'Salud, Johnny', dating the postcard 'Sept. the who? 1937'.[53]

Hughes had been drawn to Spain's plight well before he left, and his poem 'Song of Spain' (1937) was read at the combined National Negro Congress and American Committee to Aid Spanish Democracy.[54] Arriving in Barcelona from Paris by train, Hughes and fellow correspondent the Cuban poet Nicholás Guillén arrived a day after a harrowing attack on the city that killed around one hundred people. Headlines on his first day read AIR RAID OVER BARCELONA, and this piece of press immediately made its way into the title of Hughes's poem, where the 'nightmare dream' comes in the form of 'The siren/ Of the air raid sounds'.[55] Perhaps his most poignant poem from his time in Spain, most of which was written during his first few weeks in the country, 'Moonlight in Valencia: Civil War', personalized a death that was no longer heroic and idealized as civilians imagined: 'An officer in a pretty uniform/ Or a nurse in a clean white dress'. Instead, night raids in the moonlight dropped bombs that left 'steel in your brain'.[56]

Wisely drafting a will before he left, Hughes faced dangers that were very real, and he 'was lucky not to have been killed himself'.[57] He missed being 'blasted out of a Brigade battalion's new field headquarters', barely escaped a hand grenade that fell within 'feet' of him, but in the end sustained only one minor wound. It occurred not when he 'dodged the line of sniper fire', but when a bullet nicked him in the elbow when he was in the streets of Madrid's University City.[58] Riding in military convoys, Hughes befriended one of the drivers, and Bernard 'Bunny' Rucker gave Hughes the best coat he had yet owned. Hughes was still wearing it to a poetry reading when the two met three years later in Columbus, Ohio.[59]

Hughes joked that 'During the months that I was in Spain I became acquainted with more white American writers than at any other time of my life.'[60] Though John Dos Passos had left before Hughes arrived, he met Dorothy Parker, Stephen Spender and W. H. Auden. Hughes spent an entire day speaking privately with Ernest Hemingway, but quietly reserved the right to withhold exactly what formidable topics their intimate discussions covered. Now turning his own wisp of a moustache into the full thickness of Papa's, Hughes was clearly impressed by Hemingway saying: 'I found him a big likeable fellow whom the men in the Brigades adored.'[61] Hughes had lost over 6 kilograms (14 lb) by the end of his six months in Spain. He was 'hungry' but never 'bored'.[62] Hemingway threw a farewell party for Hughes in Madrid. It started only after one of the 'heaviest shelling attacks on the city' finally ended, leaving a very drunk poet stumbling with Guillén to a bus that sped them to Valencia.[63]

Returning from Spain, Hughes founded his own personal playhouse when he started the Harlem Suitcase Theater. On opening night, 21 April 1938, an overflow crowd of two hundred people paid a dollar to see his play *Don't You Want to Be Free* performed with so few props that everything could be 'packed into a suitcase' and staged almost without a budget.[64] It built on many Russian experimental techniques and was New York's first 'theatre-in-the-round, a new form widely adopted in later years'.[65] Thirty-eight performances and 3,500 people later, the inaugural season closed, prompting Hughes to use this play to launch similar theatre groups in four additional cities including Chicago and Los Angeles.[66] The play itself was mounted in Atlanta, New Orleans and Nashville, and Hughes was glad to thank Louise Thompson for inspiring him to write it.[67] Performed over 135 times in two years, *Don't You Want to Be Free* became the longest-running play in Harlem during Hughes's lifetime.[68] The lyrical play featured a 'majestic youth' reading Hughes's poem 'Negro' as well as Toy Harper presenting a moving rendition of 'The Negro Mother'.[69]

The Harlem Suitcase Theater ended its second season in stirring fashion with performances of a poem that sought to help commute the sentence of a man expecting to be executed. Still cognizant of the fate of the Scottsboro Boys since they were first falsely imprisoned in 1931, Hughes penned one of his longer poems, 'August 19th', when the death sentence was reconfirmed upon Clarence Norris on 16 June 1938. Clarence was the only man still sentenced to death in the Scottsboro Case, so Hughes took up lobbying for his life when he used the date set for his execution as both refrain and title. The poem was likely performed at the theatre by Robert Earl Jones, father of the famous James Earl Jones who would become the unmistakable voice of Darth Vader and spokesman for CNN.[70] The poem included clear directives from Hughes: 'Read this poem aloud and think of young Clarence Norris pacing his lonely cell in the death house in Alabama, doomed to die on August 19th . . . punctuate this poem with a single drumbeat after each line: "August 19th is the date." Like the beat of doom.'[71]

Like the upcoming change in Norris's fate, the poem itself went through some unique transformations as it went into publication for the 28 June 1938 edition of the *Daily Worker*. Unlike Hughes's earlier drafts, the extra words 'Scottsboro Death Date' were dropped from the title. Moreover, Hughes's 'August 19th' was actually published merely as 'August 19', and line twenty received added quotation marks around 'law' in the version published in this newspaper. Line 94 was changed to a lower case 'h' in the second appearance of 'honorable So-and-So'. Perhaps the copy-editors at the paper wanted to maintain consistency with the quotation marks as Hughes had placed 'by law' within quotations earlier in the poem. However, the shift to a lower case 'honorable' after an upper case 'Honorable' appeared earlier in line six of Hughes's work suggests the proofreading was rushed to place Hughes's poem into print.[72]

The editors also might not have understood what Hughes was doing in his poem and therefore made choices without realizing some of the more poetic elements at work in 'August 19th'. An extended examination of these variations reveals meanings that have unfortunately been permanently removed from the poem (even to this day). Always an extremely careful proofreader, who cared immensely about what others might regard as minor subtleties, Hughes's poem is dialogic, and its multiple voices speak of events from different perspectives. Hence, local voices are told they will see a 'black boy die', but the speaker of the poem asserts a contrary fact when the original copy reads later: 'A young black-man will die.' The idea is that someone who is derogatorily being called a 'boy' is in fact a 'man'. For consistency's sake, this 'man' was changed to 'boy' in the published version. As the momentum builds in the imagined drumming of performance, Hughes tried to typologically imply increasing volume when he ended the poem with a capital 'D' in the final 'Will you let me Die?'[73] Like the earlier changes, this artist's flair is once again lost, and so the printed versions all read instead with the grammatically correct 'd' in 'die'.

Two other changes have significant consequences for understanding this poem. First, Hughes never intended any of his lines to be indented as they are in every published version. These indentations were obviously the act of the newsprint editors, who had to fit the poem into a column on page seven of their paper. However, even when later margins were wider, all future editors of the poem likewise indented lines clearly meant to continue unbroken on one line. Second, a word originally written by Hughes has been dramatically toned down. In his original copy, Hughes wrote: 'Kill all the leeches' twice in the space of three lines.[74] He was suggesting that the act of executing Norris be applied instead to the men who make such decisions, both in America against the poor and abroad, in places such as Spain and China. 'Kill' is a powerful word. While today's readers might suppose Hughes was intending to turn the tables so that those who condone such murder would pay the price of *contrapasso* as opposed to the innocent Norris, the word 'Kill' was inadvertently printed later to instead read 'stop' in both instances. Each subsequent appearance of 'stop' is not capitalized like the first words of all the rest of Hughes's lines, and it is in an odd font and size. Readers might freely imagine Hughes trying to insert the logic of a Western Union Telegram, hoping that some urgent message might come through to save Norris from being executed.

Another very likely explanation for the change could be that the word 'stop' was suggested as less violent and more acceptable, and that the word moved forward into print without ever being approved or denied by Hughes. In this way it reads as if a placeholder was published without anyone ever formally choosing it as the substitute for 'Kill'. Despite such promising imaginative possibilities, the reality is that 'Kill' did appear both times when originally published in the *Daily Worker*, and future editors substituted a word that neither Hughes nor the paper ever intended or printed. The alteration, present for whatever reason, clearly makes Hughes seem less angry than he really was.

It is worth reviewing this poem in detail because a miraculous thing happened soon after the original publication of 'August 19th'. With the poem being actively distributed throughout Birmingham, Alabama, by the Communist Party USA to raise support for the Scottsboro Defense Fund, Governor Bibb Graves commuted Clarence Norris's sentence to life in prison on 5 July 1938.[75] Hughes's poem was part of a series of earnest pleas to the governor. In fact, citizens were writing directly to Graves, and Rudolph Castown, of Staten Island, New York, had his complaint republished in the same edition of the *Daily Worker* that Hughes's poem appeared in. Castown wrote that he had heard the news in much the same way as Hughes himself: 'Press dispatches bring me to the shocking news that Clarence Norris, one of the Scottsboro boys, is to be executed on Aug. 19.'[76] With Norris personally expecting to be pardoned completely, his sentence was instead merely commuted to life in prison. This change in his destiny occurred only eight days after Hughes's poem was published, just in time to be performed anew before the Harlem Suitcase Theater season ended.[77] Hughes had originally ended the poem with this directive: 'A drum beats, louder and louder, faster and faster, like the beating of a heart.' The imagined fear of a man about to die was relevant for only eight days after its publication, so the poem was swiftly amended when Hughes added these notes in pencil: 'Then a distant voice speaks and slowly the drum dies down.'[78] Probably unconscious of the poor choice of words in 'dies down', Hughes had a new ending to the poem typed that has escaped all reprinting and critical commentary on the significance of Norris's changed fate:

I hereby,
I hereby,
I hereby,
Governor Bibb Graves speaking:
I hereby commute,

Your sentence to
LIFE IMPRISONMENT.
Life . . . .
. . . . Imprisonment . . . . . .
Life . . . .
. . . . Imprisonment . . . . . .
Clarence . . . .
. . . . . . .Norris
Life . . . . . .
. . . . . Imprisonment . . . . [79]

The updated revision reveals Hughes's commitment to news that was quickly altering on its way to becoming history. The new final lines do not read as victory, but as a death deferred. Norris was eventually paroled in 1946, after which he disappeared to Harlem twice before finally being pardoned thirty years later by Governor George Wallace in 1976. Norris spent 45 years either in prison, facing the death sentence or hiding from the law for a crime he did not commit. There is no textual evidence here to suggest he was not executed based solely on the subsequent reprintings of the poem Hughes published in June 1938.

Langston Hughes's mother Carrie died on 3 June 1938, after a four-year bout with breast cancer. Hughes's relationship with Carrie had been strained. Having essentially left Hughes to be raised by his grandmother Mary until he was fourteen, or left completely alone (as he had been during his high school years in Cleveland), she also imagined what many others wrongly suspected: she felt that because her son was famous, he must also be rich. Despite the fact that Hughes often lived from publication to publication, she consistently pestered him for money without even the pretence of reimbursement. Hughes often complied, sending cash to aid her needs, yet even in a letter confirming his recent gift of $30, he was chided when he read

'I'd love to have you just a little while once in my life.'[80] Part of her justification came in her following complaint that 'Mother's Day came and I got no card . . . No one remembered me.'[81]

Nonetheless, his mother influenced his writing of *Not Without Laughter* (1930) as the three main female characters – Tempy, Annjee and Harriett – can be understood as all emphasizing different key traits of her personality.[82] Representative of her struggles, Carrie had written about a plan she had: 'Say here in Cleveland Antiques are all the rage and I was just wondering if we could not sell the Harper's [*sic*] Ferry Shawl? Do you know where it is? A man told me here last week I ought to get $500.00 for it.'[83] Hughes had been told that the shawl, bullet-ridden and bloodstained, had been worn proudly by his grandmother's first husband, Lewis Leary, who died at the raid on Harpers Ferry in 1859.[84] Wrapped in this shawl when he slept at night as a child, it took on remarkable symbolic significance to Hughes, who thoughtfully stored it and never dreamed of selling it. Owning a personal photo of Leary, Hughes eventually donated the shawl to the Ohio Historical Society.

Growing up, Leary had been educated by private tutors and even waited upon by black servants, some of whom were slaves. A family myth asserted that he left his home in Fayetteville, North Carolina, after knocking a white overseer to the ground; however, his departure seems to have instead revolved around his black father's hypocritical 'indulgence in slavery'.[85] Leaving without a single word spoken to his wife about his plans, Leary set off to fight with John Brown trying to free Virginia's slaves. Holed up in a rifle factory, repelling at least six attacks on its armory, he eventually fled through the back door only to face the swift current of the Shenandoah River, where he 'managed to reach a rock outcropping in mid-river, where he was "shot through the body" and collapsed'. Dragged to shore and nearly lynched, he suffered in agony for another 'ten or twelve hours before succumbing to his wounds'.[86]

The shawl, dyed yellow with walnuts or dandelions and blue from indigo after being spun on a 'walking' wheel, may have been presented to Hughes's grandmother Mary Langston at a Christmas Day commemoration ceremony held in Oberlin in 1859.[87] Modern examination reveals that wear and moths are responsible for the holes in the cloth with 'no signs of either bullet holes or bloodstains' anywhere to be found.[88] Unknown to Hughes or any of his previous biographers, it is now clear that 'the story that this shawl was at the battle of Harpers Ferry is not true'.[89]

Instead, the shawl was a fitting symbol as the men did indeed wear dull brown shawls on arrival, and many of the dead raiders were found to be buried in shawls when exhumed years later. The misattributed symbol held much deserved meaning for Hughes and his family. In fact, it had actually been Mary's second husband, Charles Langston, who delivered the stirring speech that first 'gave Brown the idea of recruiting troops in Oberlin'.[90]

Always close to his sense of personal identity, Hughes memorialized the acts of the 22 men when he wrote 'October 16: The Raid' (1931). While Hughes chose to valorize John Brown himself in the poem, the memory of Lewis Leary is embedded in the place of Harpers Ferry itself as Hughes recalls those buried in the ground in a space still 'alive with ghosts today'.[91]

Langston Hughes became the first African American to write a Hollywood screenplay when, in the spring of 1939, he joined Clarence Muse and began an eight-week project on location with high hopes that he had 'an opportunity to transform the image of black Americans in movies'. Early signs were encouraging when the two writers read producer Sol Lesser's early directives: 'Messrs. Hughes and Muse are to be given the utmost liberty in developing the Second Draft Screenplay, so that it will contain every element of their conception of the story.'[92] Slowly through the process, innovative cultural portrayals eventually gave way to stereotypical depictions of black life in antebellum Louisiana so that on many fronts Hughes was publicly embarrassed after its screening.

Though others would note that the B-movie slipped in 'subversive truths', such as an auction scene that was 'pointedly represented', many of Hughes's friends on the left were bewildered at the final product.[93] Louise Thompson brought up the reaction cautiously, writing with a sense of duty that 'I should have told you the word that is going around.'[94] Paid $500 for his screenplay (about $8,000 (£6,500) in today's economy), and given full credit for two of the film's songs, Hughes used the Hollywood money to pay his mother's funeral bills, doctor's bills 'in Cleveland and New York', and to fund the first new suits, shirts and shoes he had bought in three years.[95] Another $100 went to outstanding debts to friends as well as paying back loans on old membership dues so that for the first time in years Hughes could write 'I see my debts dwindling steadily.'[96] What money left was set aside to fund his next writing project. Despite its hundreds of appearances, his radical play *Don't You Want to Be Free* had resulted in royalties of only $40, not nearly enough to even cover his own expenses in writing it.[97] Now famous and poor, and not yet forty years old, Langston Hughes was poised to recount it all in his first autobiography.

To Carl —
Sincerely —
Langston

In December 1941, Hughes had a number of portraits taken by Gordon Parks that brought the photographer greater artistic credibility, and some of these images were autographed for close friends, such as Carl Van Vechten.

6

Aimee B. Simple, 1940–45

Hughes's first autobiography, *The Big Sea*, was finished in the comfort of Noël Sullivan's California farm in Hollow Hills. After enjoying total seclusion in Chicago's Hotel Grand, he arrived in California having started the project the previous May.[1] As he once told fellow African American writer Richard Wright, 'Six months in one place is long enough to make one's life complicated.'[2] Back in Carmel-by-the-Sea, Hughes spent evenings talking with a cigarette dangling customarily from the left side of his mouth to be sure his words always came out right. He also gained more than 5 kilograms (12 lb) enjoying the comforts of working in isolation near a pear orchard, fireplace and patio.[3] These were comforts he once again needed as he pawned his suit, borrowed $400 to hire a typist and paid overdue rent back in Harlem.[4] Soon to be named by the *Amsterdam News* as one of New York's most 'eligible bachelors', Hughes was 'likeable, conscientious, but somehow enveloped in a thin cloud of mystery'.[5] Readers were anxious to peak behind the veil.

Hughes explained genuinely that his writing process was spontaneous, something that happens 'right away', and 'if there is a chance to put the poem down then, I write it down . . . for poems are like rainbows: they escape you quickly.'[6] Without his correspondence, stored back in Harlem, Hughes wrote the prose account from memory. Once finished, Carl Van Vechten again took Hughes's titanic effort up with Blanche Knopf, asserting that rather than cutting long sections about the Harlem Renaissance, this era's subject-matter should be expanded. Despite her personal objections, she relented when Van Vechten rightly called Hughes 'the last historian of the period who really knows anything about it'.[7] In the end, Hughes produced an original source that has stood 'unsurpassed' for its 'insight and information on the age'.[8]

Confession and bitterness were absent from a genre where the first is often expected and the second was inconspicuous to most white readers, who were waiting for examples of racism or frustrations about unequal opportunity or pay. Hughes instead went 'paddling nonchalantly on its surface – just as millions of blacks passed through their lives under the most degrading circumstances by enduring and smiling and laughing, and thus preserved a fundamental sense of dignity and self-respect'.[9] In a narrative where it was easy to mistake the mask for a face, Hughes built his story around three episodes that served as 'pillars' for the story. He carefully linked the tears he shed after his inability to see Jesus at the altar in his youth with his debilitating response to his father and equally painful break with Godmother.[10] In place of his church conversion, Hughes symbolically wrote of his first experience crossing the equator, where he was 'baptized in salt water' by a 'carpenter, in a wooden crown and a false beard'.[11]

Hughes also omitted a distinct feature of his identity as his allies on the left directly noted 'not a single mention of a radical publication you've written or a single radical you have met or has meant anything to you'.[12] Perhaps the Soviet-Nazi non-aggression pact, signed while he was writing, had affected this choice as ties with the USSR were now visibly placing Russia and its supporters on the wrong side of history. The location itself, writing where the Vigilantes had run him out of town five years earlier, or expectations from both the publisher and audience Hughes was seeking, might have swayed this glaring omission as well.

Reviews were very positive when the book appeared in August 1940, with the *New York Times* promoting its release and *Newsweek*

calling it 'the most readable book of the year'.[13] *The Big Sea* would
not be the runaway success of the year though, as Richard Wright's
stirring novel *Native Son* was both a critical success and a bestseller.
With his novel's tantalizing sexual descriptions and violent murder
plot, Wright had sensationalized the very south side of Chicago
where Hughes himself had earlier planned to write his own novel.
Hughes's project faltered when his mother's illness drained both
his time and the resources from the $1,500 Guggenheim fellowship
he had been awarded for the novel in 1936. Any human being
would have felt a 'twinge of pure envy' now that Wright's 'financial
problems were solved forever'.[14] Despite such internal jealousy of
the man Hughes would refer to as the 'sepia Steinbeck' in jest among
close friends, Wright and Hughes would always remain very close.[15]
Each reviewed the other's work favourably, and Hughes gladly
assisted him as he did all unknown writers, having 'personally
introduced [Ralph] Ellison to Richard Wright and the rest of the
left' in 1936.[16] Wright and Hughes collaborated for the only time
in their careers on 'Red Clay Blues' (1939), a poem where Hughes's
blues style captures the thoughts of a speaker who longs to return
to his Georgia farm, hoping a 'big storm starts to blow' to remove
the current landlord.[17]

Promoting *The Big Sea* in Pasadena, California, Hughes had
anticipated sales of over one hundred copies from an audience
expected to reach five hundred at the plush Vista del Arroyo Hotel.
He had of course by now mastered carrying his cigarette in his left
hand, ever ready to take up a pen and sign his name with the right.
Amelia Earhart's widower, retired publisher George Palmer Putnam,
had invited Hughes as the guest of honour at a gala luncheon on
15 November. Suddenly, before the event began, 'God Bless America'
could be heard blaring from a convoy of cars carrying over a hundred
angry protesters.[18] Members of the Four Square Gospel Church
arrived to picket the author's appearance, induced by their leader
Aimee Semple McPherson, who would denounce Hughes as 'a red

devil in black skin' from the pulpit at her 5,000-seat Angelus Temple until her death in 1944.[19] Hughes had come to her attention when she was named in his poem 'Goodbye Christ' as representing one among many religious leaders who had 'made too much money' from the Bible and 'pawned' Christ until he had 'done wore out' his relevance.[20] In the poem, Marx, Lenin and Stalin are named as the best contemporary replacements in a poem even more explosive than 'Good Morning Revolution' (1932) and 'Christ in Alabama' (1931) combined.

McPherson built one of the first megachurches in America, and her followers were handing out leaflets with Hughes's poem and the words: 'ATTEND THE LUNCHEON CHRISTIANS . . . *and eat if you can*'.[21] Worse, protesters shouted 'Down where I come from, we don't shake hands with niggers.'[22] With Hughes himself now cancelling the event to try and save the hotel further embarrassment, he was escorted away in a car by the chief of police, whose officers had genuinely tried to dissuade the protesters by issuing traffic citations.[23]

Hughes had written the explosive poem in 1932 in Russia, where, without Hughes's consent, communist Otto Huiswoud 'somehow obtained the poem' and had it published immediately in Germany's *Negro Worker*. Never before had there been 'a literary work by an African American that had proven to be so controversial among African Americans'.[24] Haunting Hughes for the rest of his career, the *Saturday Evening Post* quickly seized upon an opportunity, knowing Hughes had also named them in his poem. The *Post* printed 'Goodbye Christ', stunning Hughes when he found himself face to face with the poem as he held his copy of the 21 December 1940 edition.[25] This Christmas edition was the magazine's most widely circulated publication of the year.

Trying to ease damage that could not be undone, Hughes worried for the sponsors of an upcoming lecture and recital combination featuring himself and Ivan Browning, an entertainer who starred in both the Broadway production of *Shuffle Along* (1921) and later appeared frequently on the popular TV show *Amos and Andy* in the 1950s.[26] Faced with public ostracism, one of the things he feared most in life, Hughes then made the regrettable mistake of apologizing for the poem rather than defending it. Hughes could have followed the lead of poet Melvin Tolson, who had earlier defined the poem by declaring that 'Jesus was a "radical" and a "Socialist" whose "guns were turned on Big Business and religionists".'[27] This tact would also have placed Hughes well within many actual Church teachings of the era, as African Methodist Episcopal (AME) minister D. Ormonde Walker had long been declaring 'Jesus gave communism to the world before Marx, Lenin, or Stalin.'[28] Missing the opportunity to instruct the uninformed public about how the poem should be read, Hughes instead offered a press release on New Year's Day 1941 in which he tried to explain the contrasting liberty he witnessed in Russia when compared with the American injustice surrounding the Scottsboro Boys. Without lynchings and segregation, the poem's collective 'I' represented all the Marxists who believed in the Soviet dream. Hughes finished with what read as an apology, asserting that he had 'left the terrain of "the radical at twenty" to approach the "conservative at forty"'.[29] To his many friends on the left, the statement itself was ironic, being written in response to a poem 'intended to attack hypocrisy'.[30] Genuinely overwhelmed by the controversy, Hughes wrote to Louise Thompson that 'it'll probably take me until 1942 to recover.'[31] In fact the poem would haunt him for the next two decades upon swiftly being added to his FBI file.

Hughes learned that his poems were being translated throughout Brazil. At this time, he also started to learn that some friends preferred he 'sing' rather than 'complain'.[32] Hughes did both; racism served as an everyday theme for him both before and after America's involvement in the Second World War. Without his knowing, his poems were secretly published in Dutch as *Lament for Dark Peoples*

(1944), to serve as a rebellious weapon against the Nazi occupation of Holland.[33] He also privately met his leftist friends' wishes, writing to Louise Thompson's newborn child 'by the time you are a big girl, I hope the red star will be shining everywhere.'[34] Having personally experienced what it was to be shut out from any real control, both on Broadway and in Hollywood, Hughes published the poem 'Note on Commercial Theatre' (1940) to lament how black culture and its art had been appropriated. In often cited lines, Hughes accused such invisible producers, directors and lyricists by writing: 'you fixed 'em/ So they don't sound like me./ Yep, you done taken my blues and gone.'[35] With an idealism fuelled by innocence, Hughes's speaker asserts that the clearest remedy to this commodification is to write the plays, scripts and songs himself. What Hughes himself failed to ever fully grasp is that, unlike his books and essays, the world of Hollywood and Broadway never allots anyone full control, regardless of race.

Even when Japanese aggression brought the United States into the war, Hughes continued to find the same real-life ironies in his poetry that he always uncovered. 'Merry-Go-Round' (1942) exposes the illogic of segregation by voicing the genuine confusion of a child who is unsure where she is allowed to sit. The child, whom Hughes always referred to as a girl when introducing the poem, knows that she is supposed to sit apart from whites, but she is paralysed because the ride offers neither a front nor back. In the end, the child innocently asks: 'Where's the horse/ For a kid that's black?'[36] In the poem, the child is 'inadvertently teaching a white man the rules of segregation' and the poem ends without an answer to the question 'as if no sound logic for segregation's principles can be offered'.[37]

The advent of the Second World War heightened Hughes's call for double victory. If racism was to be fought overseas, the battle should first be won at home. No word summed up this plea for Hughes more than 'freedom'. He penned a song recorded by Josh White called 'Freedom's Road' (1942), explaining to Noël Sullivan that 'We all want to beat Hitler and we all want to march down Freedom Road. But that road will have to run past Roland [Hayes]'s farm, too. Else it won't really be going anywhere – for anybody.'[38] With the famous singer recently beaten up in a Georgia store after a dispute, headlines about Hayes served as a reminder of American racism. In the poem 'Refugee in America' (1943), he wrote that freedom was on his heart 'all day everyday', and that coupled with 'liberty', would 'almost make me cry'.[39] Hungry for freedom to arrive, Hughes asserted in yet another poem, 'Freedom' (1943), the unforgettable statement: 'I do not need freedom when I'm dead./ I cannot live on tomorrow's bread.'[40]

The concept of 'freedom' made an even longer appearance when Hughes wrote 'Freedom's Plow' (1943), his longest poem to date, at the request of Lester B. Granger, executive secretary of the National Urban League. Several members of the organization helped Hughes shape the text that Broadway star Paul Muni read to music on NBC radio on 15 March 1943.[41] Hughes would publish the piece as a stand-alone book and sell it for 10 cents at his poetry readings, and it was later performed publicly by actor Fredric March.[42] The poem itself told the history of America from an African American perspective, filling its lines with the hope and promises made in the Declaration of Independence. However, its roots were spiritual and temporal. At the time, the United Nations had formed the year before with its primary mission being a collaborative world stance against the Axis powers. Its first declaration was immediately signed by 26 nations, with another 22 adding their names the next day. With its headquarters in New York, this new breed of global hope is what Hughes alludes to in the poem when he writes of 'men united as a nation'. Hughes knew America is a dream, and he extended that hope to the world across geopolitical lines:

Thus the dream becomes not one man's dream alone,
But a community dream.

Not my dream alone, but *our* dream.
Not my world alone,
But *your world and my world*,
Belonging to all the hands who build.[43]

To deepen the identity of all those working hands, Hughes built
his poem around the lyrics of a song concurrently being revitalized
from an old Negro spiritual. The poem's refrain, '*Keep Your Hand on
the Plow!*', came from a song that had been around long before its
first documentation in 1917.

Hughes began writing a weekly column for the *Chicago Defender*
in late November 1942. With a primarily African American
readership, Hughes called the paper 'the journalistic voice of
a largely voiceless people'.[44] Though its reporting sometimes
embraced the sensationalism often associated with the 'yellow
journalism' of the age, the paper's reach was far and wide. It was
distributed across the country, and many of Hughes's articles
were picked up by other African American outlets. Hughes would
continue to write weekly for the *Defender* for the next 22 years.
Always wanting to please the public, his only stipulation in
accepting the offer was that he be assigned an assistant to respond
to each and every piece of post he received.

His column was called 'Here to Yonder', and Hughes immediately
took satirical stances on a variety of key issues. To those who feared
what an end to segregation might lead to, Hughes quipped that he
already knew as 'The millions of mulattos in the South today are
living proof of integration.' To those who feared intermarriage
Hughes proposed the simplest of solutions: 'The way to integrate
without intermarriage is for the girl to decline.'[45] In the middle of
the war effort of 1942, readers could not help but laugh when the
author informed them that blacks who could pass for white had
been donating their blood to the Red Cross in order to save lives.
Because the organization had a policy of segregating its blood bank,

Hughes wryly reminded them that those who inadvertently accepted such transfusions were forever changed because 'one drop of black blood makes a man black in the South.'[46]

On writing about a former black soldier who struck a white man and was then sent to prison, Hughes detailed the life of a man who had survived 'the dangers of the South Pacific all right, but here in our own Dixieland, Jim Crow got the best of him'. Hughes suggested the excessive discrimination he felt led to a 'segregation-fatigue' that was running so rampant it might be termed 'Jim Crow shock'.[47]

Having avoided or overcome shell shock, blacks were also regularly refused admittance into American hospitals. Hughes devoted an entire article to document this plight, which affected Jeffrey Jennings, Juliette Derricotte and blues-great Bessie Smith. Though he could have listed many others, including boxer Jack Johnson's demise in North Carolina, he concluded that 'even inanimate perishable freight from an overturned truck might, in wind and storm, be given emergency shelter in a white hospital corridor or garage – but not bleeding, breathing men and women who happen to be black.'[48]

Hughes created one of the most endearing characters in all of literature when he introduced readers to a 'simple minded friend' in this column on 13 February 1943. The character was named Jesse B. Semple in 1945, the spelling of 'simple' with an 'e' being not so much an easy pun as a choice likely to undermine Aimee Semple McPherson, who died the year before. The character came to be referred to merely as 'Simple', and his arguments with Hughes himself slowly gave way to an educated man named 'Boyd' serving as foil instead.[49] The dialogic nature of the back and forth allowed Hughes to 'convey the particular experience of being black in America while retaining the emotional distance that fiction allows'.[50] Simple was based on an actual man whom Hughes serendipitously joined for a drink at Patsy's Bar and Grill not far from his Harlem residence. As Hughes sipped his standard gin and tonic, the man comically found himself in a playful argument with his wife about his factory job. Hughes immediately started writing detailed notes that became the basis for the character.[51]

As Simple's life grew, he took on a wife (Joyce) as well as a girlfriend (Zarita), thus allowing Hughes to develop the piece into a full ensemble. By 1948 comedians were 'borrowing' material from Hughes's column for use in their routines.[52] Even more humorously, Hughes started receiving post from those who genuinely assumed his characters were real. As just one example, a woman who sympathized with Joyce competing against Zarita for Simple's attention sent a 'handmade brassiere and panty set, with red bedroom slippers . . . so could "fight fire with fire"'.[53] Simple columns were eventually gathered into five full collections of material and translated into more than six languages as they sold in book form throughout the 1950s. The character also carried a play entitled *Simply Heavenly*, running for 62 performances on Broadway in 1957 and then televised as a week-long event in December 1959.[54] By 1965 New York banks were even issuing calendars with proverbs by Simple mimicking the tradition of Benjamin Franklin's Poor Richard.[55]

Hughes continued to turn his attention to songs and numerous radio plays, earning pay while he supported the war effort with his art. He wrote *John Henry Hammers It Out*, with Paul Robeson performing on the radio broadcast. Robeson had also taken the lead role in Hughes's earlier *For This We Fight*, showcased at a sold-out Negro Freedom rally at Madison Square Garden.[56] Years later, in 1952, more than 18,000 people would be there again to hear Josh White sing Hughes's 'The Ballad of Harry Moore'. Not all of his radio work escaped censorship during the war; *The Organizer*, *Brothers* and *Pvt. Jim Crow* were never aired due to Hughes daring to link 'German racism with what was happening in America'.[57] As Hughes wrote to his agent, 'God knows we better win before Hitler comes over here to aid with the lynchings!'[58]

7

F. B. Eyes, 1945–50

Hughes's writing would continue to impact generations beyond him – generations who sometimes did not even know whose words they were enjoying. For example, at the New York jazz club the Village Vanguard in early 2017, a music critic noted that one of the highlights of upcoming star Cecile McLorin Salvant's performance came when the singer 'unfolded' a 'tune over the course of 10 minutes, as the saga of an entire life: a child's promise of bright days ahead, a love that blossoms and fades, babies who wrap "a ring around a rosy" and then move away'. He noted that 'When she sang "It looks like something awful happens/ in the kitchens/ where women wash their dishes," her plaintive phrasing transformed a description of domestic obligation into genuine tragedy. A hush washed over the room.'[1] The song was 'Somehow I Never Could Believe'. Though the reviewer attributed the song to Elmer Rice, Kurt Weil composed the music. Unknown to listeners and readers of the *New Yorker*, Langston Hughes had written its lyrics fifty years before this New York crowd was moved to silence by his words.

To his stunned surprise, Hughes received a telegram from Elmer Rice in August 1945 inviting him to discuss something very mysterious. When Hughes called the next day, Rice asked if Hughes was interested in the idea of reviving Rice's 1929 Pulitzer Prize-winning play *Street Scene*. Having enjoyed the original play as well as the film, Hughes accepted the invitation of being asked to work with two white writers, knowing these circumstances were 'so remarkable as to be virtually without parallel'.[2] With 24 plays to his name, Rice was a top-tier dramatist. Weil wanted Hughes to write lyrics that 'lift the everyday language of the people into a simple, unsophisticated poetry'. Meeting in Rockefeller Center, Hughes learned the catch: he was guaranteed nothing except the chance 'to try out for the position as lyricist'. By autumn, after submitting numerous samples, he had eventually won their approval, entering into a formal contract that would pay him $750 up front with an additional 2 per cent of the weekly box-office gross.[3]

The promise of a big pay day seemed finally at hand for a writer so simultaneously smitten with the stage and consistently rebuked that he had once complained of wasting many hours 'writing for the theatre and getting nowhere', so that he now preferred 'literature between book covers'.[4] Feeling for years as if he had been 'blacklisted from birth' and doomed to have nothing more than pockets filled with manuscripts, Hughes jumped into rehearsals, rewrites and the weekly replacement of abandoned songs until rehearsals started in the autumn of 1946.[5] However, the play flopped in Philadelphia, ending up $170,000 in debt after a heavily critiqued and poorly attended three-week run. When Kurt Weil set out for the 9 January 1947 opening on Broadway he felt as though 'I were on my way to the scaffold.'[6] With significant dialogue and staging adjustments made to the play by a host of others including Oscar Hammerstein II, the play was now conversely met with thunderous applause. Virtually none of Hughes's lyrics had been changed from the Philadelphia debacle. Moreover, a song that was entirely Hughes's idea called 'Moon Faced, Starry Eyed' was hailed as the best song of the Broadway season.

After 148 shows Hughes had made over $10,000 before the play had even travelled through Europe, by far the most money he would ever earn. Still knowing that 'my public sends me a good deal of affection, my publishers so few checks', Hughes had one goal for his payout: he bought his first home.[7] Hughes would own the now famous 20 East 127th Street address in Harlem through a joint venture with Emerson and Toy Harper. Joining a couple who had become like family since renting together in Harlem seven years earlier, Hughes would live at this new home with the musician and his seamstress wife until he died. The Langston Hughes Project is currently working to preserve the home. But when the Broadway crowd was eerily quiet on opening night, sitting on their hands, waiting for something to energize them, Polyna Stoska's version of 'Somehow I Never Could Believe' brought the first cheers with a zeal that carried all the way through to the end of the crucial debut.[8]

Though Hughes had written in his short story 'Little Old Spy' (1941) about being under local surveillance when he travelled to Cuba in 1930, the intense degree to which the FBI marked his movements was mostly unknown to him. In the early part of the 1940s Hughes was placed on the FBI's '"Custodial Detention" list, an index of prominent dissidents subject to summary arrest and military confinement in case of national emergency'.[9] Along with many other African Americans, Hughes's passport was frequently reviewed to confirm the very real prospect of 'global surveillance or national house arrest'.[10] As early as 1943, FBI agents began 'sneaking into his poetry readings' as Hughes's 'contributions to the black press in particular continued to hammer FBI anticommunism'.[11]

Hughes's FBI file would be the source of formal attacks made against him in the House of Representatives in 1944, on the floor of the Senate in 1948 and in the press, when *Life* magazine published his photo in 1949 with many other communist 'dupes and fellow travelers'.[12] The FBI's attentiveness to Hughes reached the very highest level as J. Edgar Hoover's personal vendetta against the poet began after Louis Nichols stepped in to deliver one of Hoover's speeches in Evanston, Illinois, on 26 November 1947. When the speech was later requested for publication, for the first time in his life Hughes was asked to grant permission to publish 'Goodbye Christ', as the poem was used prominently in Hoover's speech. After Hughes vehemently refused, typing nearly as fast as he commonly talked, the FBI seethed at both Hughes and a publisher 'too squeamish about offending commies'. Although 'Hughes had no idea he had offended the FBI by protecting his intellectual property', Hoover and Nichols personally conspired behind the scenes to smear Hughes's name on Henry Taylor's radio show and prodded *Reader's Digest* to publish Hughes's poem. The third act of 'personal revenge' reached a climax when copies of Hughes's *Simple Speaks His Mind* (1950), on its way to becoming a bestseller, were sabotaged and mysteriously disappeared – puzzling the publisher. Despite this, it still sold 30,000 copies. However, the FBI must have been disappointed when the book's non-controversial content did not live up to the intrigue of its title.[13]

The FBI symbolically interviewed Hughes on Halloween 1950 and frequently telephoned under several different false pretences.[14] Hughes's rapid tongue must have resulted in the agents rushing through their shorthand. More damaging than such intimidation, Hoover continued to send out copies of his original speech 'Secularism—Breeder of Crime' when people contacted him seeking insight into the dangers of communism. For a full year, anyone who wrote to Hoover seeking insight into Langston Hughes received a copy of this speech where 'Goodbye Christ' had its first three full stanzas framed for all to believe Hughes was a dangerous red. After citing numerous detailed statistics on murder rates and the frequency of arrests in America, the seven-page document inaccurately contextualized Hughes's poem as 'The blasphemous utterances of one who sought public office on the ticket of the Communist Party'.[15] As William J. Maxwell has shown, this document 'effectively publicized J. Edgar Hoover as a grim-faced expert on Langston Hughes'. This extraordinary level of expertise even lasted beyond Hughes's life. In 1970, future president George H. W. Bush, then Governor of Texas, sought

Hoover's verdict when he too grew curious about 'connections Langston Hughes had with communists'.[16]

Fortunately Hughes's final two books of poems from the decade, *Fields of Wonder* (1947) and *One-way Ticket* (1949), escaped the gaze of the FBI. 'Trumpet Player' (1949) imagines the performer's mind filled with the memory of a past that extends all the way back to ancestors whipped on slave ships. Dressed in a 'fine one-button roll' and with 'vibrant hair', the music that spills from a troubled soul softens and becomes transformed as it miraculously 'Mellows to a golden note'.[17] 'Life Is Fine' (1949) parodies the rhythm and logic of the violent ending associated with singing 'Eeny, Meeny, Miny, Moe'. Invoked on playgrounds to select teams for informal games, the children's song may have originated in its most common form in New York City. In later versions, either a 'tiger' or 'nigger' is caught 'by the toe'. The idea most likely came to Hughes as Chester Himes's debut novel *If He Hollers Let Him Go* had just been published in 1945. Hughes mimics the song when he writes: 'I stood there and I hollered!/ I stood there and I cried!' He ends by asserting that the joke is on his readers because 'I'm still here livin.'[18]

Inspired by Attorney General Tom Clark, plans were set in motion in late 1947 to share America's most historic documents. Carrying either original or reproductions of the Declaration of Independence, Emancipation Proclamation, Bill of Rights and George Washington's annotated version of the Constitution, seven railcars were prepared to cover over 37,000 kilometres (23,000 mi.) in what was named The Freedom Train. To promote the venture Irving Berlin wrote a song of the same title sung by Bing Crosby and the Andrew Sisters that *Billboard* magazine believed was 'bound to latch on to the whirlpool of publicity' surrounding the grand tour.[19] As Woody Guthrie had responded earlier to Berlin's 'God Bless America' with 'This Land Is Our Land', Langston Hughes supplanted Berlin's version by countering with a song that also gained wider popularity. First printed as a poem in September 1947, to coincide with the train setting out on 17 September, the song 'The Ballad of the Freedom Train' was published by none other than W. C. Handy. With music composed by Sammy Heyward, it was later recorded by Paul Robeson and performed at numerous rallies across the country. Hughes took its title and inspiration from the Negro spiritual of the same name and, later realizing that African Americans could benefit from an alternative collection of historic materials about their freedom, he even prepared a book of his own poems on the theme using the same title.[20]

The Freedom Train encountered a substantive challenge to its proposed schedule as citizens in the South soon wondered if their experience would be segregated. In Memphis the mayor demanded that blacks view the contents at alternative hours. In Oklahoma City, one hundred singers refused to sing when their performance was not integrated into the opening ceremonies. Hattiesburg, Mississippi, had their visit withdrawn. Revised later, Hughes's poem

Ever popular with children, Hughes signs autographs in Atlanta during a book tour in 1947.

documents this: 'When it stops in Mississippi will it be made plain/ Everybody's got a right to board the Freedom Train?'[21]

Birmingham, Alabama, concocted their own plan. Because the train was seven cars long, they would admit blacks *after* an all-white group had moved into the second car, alternating car by car in something that made a farce of the freedom suggested in the very documents themselves. The 'Birmingham Plan' was enacted in at least seven other cities throughout the South. With a pencil in his hand, Hughes underlined the line below when he read in a summary of such activities that: 'In Augusta, Ga., however, it was reported that there was no separation of Negros and whites, and no racial conflicts occurred.'[22] In writing Birmingham into his poem, Hughes had rightly asked: 'They even got a segregated lane./ Is that the way to get aboard the Freedom train?'[23]

The musical composer William Grant Still believed he would be a perfect complement to the experienced dramatic skills of Langston Hughes. The two men began discussing turning one of Hughes's plays into an opera as early as October 1936.[24] Hughes had begun drafting ideas for a play about Haiti's 1791 revolution for independence on 19 September 1928. Originally titled *Emperor of Haiti*, the play was eventually developed into an opera with Still titled *Troubled Island*. The plot centres around the efforts of Jean Jacques Dessalines to free his country from French colonial rule. The work was last staged as a play with Hughes in attendance on 9 May 1948, and it finally reached the stage transformed into an opera in 1949. The eventual staging of the opera was fraught with a mesmerizing number of stops and starts.

As an avowed anti-communist, Still made for a rather interesting counter to Hughes. Hughes created the entire script on his own for two reasons. First, he wanted to celebrate the Haitian revolution understood so well by his relatives. Second, he used this event as a veil for his 1930s desire to inspire something of the same in America. Still either missed or consciously chose to ignore the historical and political implications of the play when he wrote: 'the rebellion is used merely as exposition. In substance, it's a love story.'[25] Hughes stated things very differently, seeing his play as 'being based on man's eternal fight for freedom'.[26] One thing the two men agreed on was how to handle the principal song of the play: Hughes's 'I Dream a World'. Compliant in every regard, Hughes promised Still as early as January 1940 that he would hold the centrepiece of the opera under tight veil even when he personally wanted to pass it on to Paul Robeson.[27]

By all accounts the performance of Hughes's 'I Dream a World' was one of the songs Still himself most admired in *Troubled Island*. During auditions, Still noted that 'the Martel is a very fine singer'.[28] The singer of Hughes's aria, Oscar Natzka, was again singled out for voluntary praise, as Still wrote to his wife twelve days later: 'The Bass has a most remarkable voice.'[29] Years later, with the bitter defeat of the opera's truncated run continuing to inform every aspect of his life, Still could not refrain from lauding Natzka's singing: 'I don't know of anyone else who would have fit the role better than he.'[30]

In the recording made from the opening night performance of the opera, it is clear that no other point in the entire opera stirs the crowd to more sonorous applause than what occurs immediately after Natzka sings Hughes's 'I Dream a World'. Natzka's rendition runs just short of two full minutes. To capture some of the sounds reminiscent of Haitian dialect, he rolls no less than eight different 'r' sounds that appear in words such as dream, freedom, greed, race, every and free. He reserves his most expressive rolling 'r' near the end when he reaches 'wretchedness'. With a heavenly harp strumming softly three times in the middle of the aria, Natzka turns Hughes's original 'will' into 'shall' for the only variation in diction from Hughes's original, then repeats the final line 'my world!' three consecutive times. The immediate applause comes at a point in the opera where no pause in the action is intended.

Although this was not even so much as a scene break, the aria received a full eight seconds of sustained applause on the tape of the performance. But even this time has been cut as the sound can be heard fading out at the end of this applause and Jean Jacques' next lines signal a literal restart of both the action and the recording. The surviving tape has clearly edited out much of this unexpected ovation, and it is ultimately unclear just how long it washed over the theatre.[31] It was precisely because of this kind of moment that Hughes opened a bottle of 'Barbancourt rum from Haiti that he had been saving' to celebrate opening night.[32]

Revered by a sold-out audience that gave the opera a staggering 22 consecutive curtain calls, it was Still who took his bows while Hughes remained seated in the audience on opening night.[33] Although formally scheduled to appear only two more times, on 10 April and 1 May, the opera was quietly expected to return on unannounced dates in the near future and run for much longer than Hughes's short ties of the era. Why was an opera whose opening night performance met with unquenchable applause ultimately unable to sustain a run of more than three performances?

If the critics were to be trusted, and Still did not believe they should be, many of them found little originality in the musical compositions themselves, citing overtones of other famous composers present in the opera rather than the fresh authentic voice of Still himself.[34] In regards to the staging, Hughes's personal secretary, who deplored the dancing, overheard an audience member critique the costuming by calling the emperor's cloak a mere 'bathrobe'.[35]

As if these reasons were not enough, perhaps not so incidentally, a 'pro-Russian, pro-Leftist rally was scheduled to coincide with the opening night of *Troubled Island*'.[36] For three consecutive days leading up to the performance, a Cultural and Scientific Conference for World Peace was held nearby at the Waldorf Astoria.[37] Hughes himself was an overt sponsor of this event, which was a 'clear successor to the pro-Marxist World Congress of Intellectuals held in Wroclaw, Poland, the previous August'.[38] Hundreds of picketers lined nearby streets. Guilty by association, the Stills began receiving 'communications from Commies in different parts of the country – all asking for funds'.[39] Writing to his wife, Still exhales with relief that he was never caught on camera with his counterpart: 'How glad I am that no photos were made with Langston!'[40]

As a direct response to the conference itself, it was left to *Life* magazine to land the final blow. On 4 April 1949, a mere six days before the second scheduled performance of *Troubled Island*, *Life* ran a four-page article incriminating people it declared were intimately aligned with the communist movement. Alongside Albert Einstein, Aaron Copeland, Leonard Bernstein and Arthur Miller, Langston Hughes was pictured in a national publication that proved to be as damaging as actually setting fire to the stage, props and costumes of *Troubled Island*.[41] Who wanted to risk being subconsciously influenced or labelled a sympathizer for attending a play written by a known communist? Hughes had ended his 1948 reading tour in the summer complaining of being 'a bit weary of six months of red-baiting' only to see these same communist accusations follow him home to New York a year later.[42]

8

Montage of a Dream Deferred, 1950–53

In high demand, Hughes in 1950 was working non-stop to bring a myriad of projects to completion. For as many items as Hughes finished, three or four others went unstaged or unpublished as a reminder that he frequently took on too much. Dropping newspaper clippings onto his blankets, he often fell asleep with cheque paper clipped to some unanswered correspondence. He ended up reading each of these again when he woke after noon most days. With exceptional energy, Hughes completed an astonishing 25 poetry readings in a mere nine days travelling through North Carolina, Virginia and Maryland.[1] Writing for fifteen consecutive hours one evening, Hughes wobbled out into the streets of Harlem shocked to find it was already Saturday, and he had missed a radio appearance.[2] Combined with age, it was these hours that forced him to get glasses, and he thinned his moustache to balance against his receding hairline. His popularity continued to rise internationally as an Italian translation of *The Big Sea* was released with a cover featuring Pablo Picasso's 1925 painting *Still-life with Antique Head* (1925). With muted browns and startling whites, the cover image features two abstract figures facing each other. A book hovers in between the man and woman as ancient Greece and Africa meet through the bent neck of a lute whose frets resemble wrinkles on an elephant's trunk. *Not Without Laughter* was appearing in France, the Netherlands, Sweden and Argentina. Switzerland was publishing his short story 'Father and

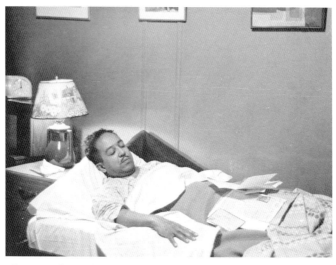

Often writing from midnight to dawn, Hughes sleeps in his home under unfinished correspondence as noon approaches in June 1949.

Son' as a small book, and Czechoslovakia brought out a version of his autobiography.

Even after all his success, some struggles were still typical for Hughes. In the summer of 1950, Hughes worked shirtless outdoors in Maine to complete another play at this time, *Just around the Corner* (1950), featuring Gene Kelley's brother. It came to nothing. Hughes worked off a $1,500 advance to write *Battle of Harlem*, attempting to ghostwrite a biography of New York City's first black police officer. He signed a screenwriter's contract as well. Just as the film and biography never came to screen or print, Hughes had been consistently throwing himself into musical failures. In 1950 alone he wrote a failed blues 'Love Can Hurt' with Juanita Hall, 'This Is My Land' with Toy Harper, and 'Hot Cinnamon' with his assistant Nate White. When 'Dorothy's Name Is Mud' (1950) paid out, Hughes's royalties totalled a mere $10.70 for his effort.[3] While Hughes himself may not even have been able to explain or defend the full motivation for such efforts, it is easy to speculate how Hughes's art might have benefitted from greater focus.

Hughes's poetic efforts would shortly become more rewarding than at any time in his career. In fact it was 1951 (not the 1920s) when Hughes would publish his most iconic book of poetry, *Montage of a Dream Deferred*. The ability to finally own his first home in 1948 allowed Hughes to see his beloved Harlem for what it had now become. There can be no doubt about the interrelatedness of these facts as Hughes started to write almost immediately after settling in to what would be his own private studio on the third floor of 20 E 127th Street. As if he could now see it all anew from this perspective, he wrote about faces that were really masking deep pains. In his poem '125th Street' (1950), outward appearances of chocolate faces and grins as wide as melons really conceal the glow of a 'jack-o'-lantern' inside.[4] Hughes seemed to be reminding outsiders that this glow was not so much a light to approach as it was a lit fuse. To insiders in the community itself the outward had

Complete with music, art and photographs of Billie Holiday and Elsie Roxborough, Hughes's new personal studio at 20 E 127th street inspired *Montage of a Dream Deferred* (1949).

always masked deeper truths, but what Hughes was seeing now was not a struggle born with a soft dignity so much as a growing rage.

In one of the very rare poems in which the poet addressed homosexuality in any form, 'Café: 3 a.m.' (1951) both sympathizes with those in the LGBTQ community and imagines that those who intently search for such evidence may have parallel desires themselves. The time of 3 a.m. is significant as it signals the kinds of criminal behaviour possible in a bar as it transitions beyond the city's official closing time.[5] In just eleven lines, the poem suggests that local detectives are searching for 'fairies' or 'degenerates'.[6] The nation's campaigns against homosexual behaviour at this time were as intense as they would ever be. In government circles, the State Department's 'purge of the perverts' boasted of firing one homosexual a day in 1950.[7] By 1952 the American Psychiatric Association officially categorized homosexuality as a 'sociopathic personality disturbance'. On the contrary, Hughes's poem asserts: 'But God, Nature,/ or somebody/ made them that way.'[8]

Recognizing nature, nurture and even the creator as possible reasons for what the tone of the poem suggests is acceptable behaviour, the poem ends by turning the investigator's gaze back on them when he playfully ponders if a policewoman should be similarly suspected of being 'lesbian'. After hours proves a time for the seemingly '"straight" to act deviantly' and 'deviants to act "normally"'.[9] In a turn-the-tables moment, everyone is watching everyone, and everybody is suspected of what happens when boundaries are being crossed. In the end, surveillance is reversed as it is the locals at the bar who are observing potential homosexuality among the vice squad. Readers are left to wonder if the look is one of mere curiosity, or personal interest, as closing time changes official investigators into potential offenders. Those searching for insights into Hughes himself find that he concealed any clear biographical hints here just as he does in his two later short stories on the same subject, 'Blessed Assurance' (1963) and 'Seven People

Dancing' (*c.* 1961). Is the subject-matter alone enough to establish what kind of circles Hughes moved in?

In this seminal *Montage* collection, dreams were once again the central motif of Hughes's poetry. As Steven Tracy has written:

> Dreams have always figured prominently in the works of Langston Hughes . . . Hughes's work is devoted to outlining, celebrating, and agitating on behalf of the dreams of the oppressed and marginalized peoples worldwide, with particular focus on the dreams of African Americans.[10]

Montage was the achievement of a great vision. To make the focus on a city rather than merely its people, the words had to ebb and flow like the rivers that created the island of Manhattan that was for Hughes a 'dream within a dream'.[11] By coining 'dream deferred', Hughes created a metaphor with such wide reach that it made its way into everyday language. As with so much of Shakespeare, 'dream deferred' slowly lost its associations with the poet himself to become a permanent addition to American vernacular, so that eventually even u.s. immigrants with 'deferred' citizenship status are referred to as 'dreamers'.

Few scholars have successfully understood Hughes's activation of the dynamic term 'montage'.[12] While montage implies tantalizing connections to film, comparing Hughes's work to that medium can perhaps best be understood as how Hughes created a production of his city that could never be made by Hollywood. However, no scholars have yet productively imagined what Hughes's sequence might look like set to film following the five specific patterns for Russian montage established by Sergei Eisenstein. In addition, the term, coming from the French 'to mount', also has avant-garde overtones related to a 'collage-aesthetic' where newsprint and other ephemera are glued, pasted and overlapped to form a statement out of what has already been discarded.[13] Equally illuminating, the term's links to creating a composite capture the importance Hughes himself placed on arrangement. His new composite image of Harlem is composed of fragments of pictures, text and music that suggest additional frames for understanding Hughes's sequence. In fact photographers also create composites by combining several pictures to exhibit and present. As we wait for film scholars to explicate what relationship Hughes's sequence has to the moving image, photography currently stands as the most accessible point of entry for interpreting Hughes's innovation in *Montage*.

The book's dedication to both Ralph and Fanny Ellison begins to activate the connections to post-war photography. Not only had Hughes welcomed Ellison to Harlem when he first appeared, the author of the soon to be published *Invisible Man* (1952) presented business cards that read simply: 'Ralph Ellison: Photographer'. More importantly, when Hughes first sought to create this project, he was surrounded by several celebrated photographers. As a result, Hughes first pitched his new idea 'down to page layouts, and specific photo choices' and signed a contract with a photographer in 1950 for his project about Harlem that he titled *Ups and Downs*.[14] The photographer who agreed was the underappreciated Marion Palfi. However, the project stalled for unknown reasons even though capturing the essence of city life in imagery was much in vogue. In fact, a year later Palfi began her own project, *In These Ten Cities*, where she 'recorded the racial discord, financial plight, and overall misery of people in cities such as Detroit and Phoenix'.[15] Without Palfi's photographs of Harlem in *Montage*, Hughes would have to rely on only his descriptions of music and imagery to show how fragments could create a picture of the whole.

Long admiring photographers and their work, and knowing many personally, Hughes's artistic engagement with photography reached its highpoint with the 1955 publication of *The Sweet Flypaper of Life*. After the photographer Roy DeCarava phoned him the previous year, Hughes kept fifty of his photographs in his studio

and made several calls trying to ensure the larger collection would
be seen. Aaron Douglas could not help organize exhibits, however,
and calls to publishers failed, citing the expected financial losses on
what each nonetheless saw as brilliant images. Only the inspired
Richard Simon suggested the idea that the photos appear in book
form with a running narrative written by the poet. Hughes and
DeCarava commenced at once with Langston writing in direct
response to the photographs themselves without any knowledge
of the real subjects. The result: none of his books were 'ever greeted
so rhapsodically'.[16] It would soon be translated into German and
French. Hughes may have also written DeCarava's successful
Guggenheim application in 1952 – a suggestion that seems likely
given its direct stipulation to capture Harlem from every angle.[17]
Hughes would continue to support DeCarava in very direct ways.
He hand-addressed many invitations to his March 1955 photo
exhibit at New York's A Photographer's Gallery on West 84th and
even personally arranged a year later for DeCarava to take images
of Count Basie's Orchestra during a rehearsal.[18]

One of the men to praise the book was an even older friend
of the poet, Henri Cartier-Bresson. On the one hand, though
knowing each other for the last thirteen years of Hughes's life,
DeCarava consistently felt he was 'waiting for his real character
to come through' when he photographed the writer.[19] On the other
hand, Cartier-Bresson's images capture the feeling of how Hughes
looked when he was all alone. They at least convey something of
how Hughes looked in private, even if they cannot fully communicate
his thoughts. From 1956 to 1957, Cartier-Bresson took better photos
of the writer than anyone ever would, including the original cover
image for his *Selected Poems* (1959). In 2002 Hughes won the Academy
of American Poets vote as the most deserving poet worthy of a u.s.
postage stamp by receiving five times the amount of votes as the
runner-up. The image selected for Hughes's stamp was one taken
by Cartier-Bresson.

The intimacy captured in his images of Hughes resulted not only because of Cartier-Bresson's immeasurable talent, but because the two had become immediate friends when meeting almost miraculously in Mexico in 1935 when the Frenchman was preparing for his first major solo exhibit. Sharing a rundown flat near the Lagunilla Market with the photographer and Mexican writer Andrés Henestrosa, Hughes passed the evenings with Cartier-Bresson as he waited for his father's estate to be settled. Renting a separate place because his father's remaining household discouraged visits from Hughes's many late-night guests, Hughes quickly accepted the cameraman's request of writing an introduction to the photography exhibit. Hughes would write of his late evenings and even a photoshoot where he accompanied Henri: 'I recall no period in my life where I had more fun with less cash.'[20] As a result the two men became close friends, and Hughes left Mexico with images the photographer took in the very courtyard where they lived. Carter-Bresson's solo exhibit in Mexico helped launch his career following his first group show three years earlier in New York. Based in Paris, Hughes stayed with Henri and his wife in 1937 and 1938, on his way in and out of Spain where he was covering its civil war. The three shared a private 55th birthday for Hughes in Harlem, and their relationship cemented when Hughes dedicated his *Simple's Uncle Sam* (1965) to the couple.

Photographer Griffith J. Davis sat in one of Hughes's classes during one of only two semesters the poet agreed to a formal teaching post. Enrolled in his creative writing class at Atlanta University in 1947, Hughes would call Davis a 'good friend of mine' after he spent time living in Hughes's Harlem home while studying journalism at Columbia University in 1948.[21] No typical student, Davis was already working for *Ebony* developing photographs for publication when he enrolled in Hughes's class, and the men collaborated on three articles for that magazine with Hughes's words pairing with the younger man's photojournalism. When Hughes was not championing DeCarava, posing for Cartier-Bresson, sitting for photographer Gordon Parks in December 1941 or teaching, working with and housing Davis, he was also unknowingly advocating for another of the most underappreciated photographers of the age.

With a published book of her work already to her name, Marion Palfi had been invited by Hughes to guest lecture to Davis and his classmates.[22] Born in Berlin to Hungarian parents in 1907, Palfi spent her whole career on the cusp of notoriety. With the death of her mother, and her father already passed, she emigrated to America in 1940, having taken up photography six years earlier. Opposing Germany's politics, she became a 'social research photographer', as she termed it, allowing her images to both document and lobby for change. Though she began as a cabaret singer, actress and model, she left success in each endeavour behind. She was writing to Hughes in March 1945 in the very month of her first solo exhibit 'Great American Artists of Minority Groups'. After being photographed by her the year before, Hughes attended the opening at the Norlyst Gallery in New York, featuring several portraits of himself, and immediately aided in selecting the photographs for the subsequent book by Arna Bontemps, *We Have Tomorrow* (1945).[23] Taking its title from the first line of Hughes's poem 'Youth', Bontemps used twelve of her photographs. Palfi would say that from 1940 to 1945 'My closest supporter . . . was Langston Hughes, the poet. I met him while I was doing the study [*Democracy in Action*], and his aunt [Toy] became my adopted mother.'[24]

After inviting her in 1948 to speak to his class in Atlanta, Hughes was trying to connect Palfi with a Swedish journalist, Eugenie Soderberg, two years later. His strategy was to follow the same pattern he would eventually use for DeCarava's breakthrough. He started by simply keeping her images at hand and showing them to everyone he could. By 1952, from 413 E 72nd Street, Palfi was now addressing him in typed letters with 'Dearest Lang'. She told him about her frustrations in publishing her powerful photographs taken in Irwinton, Georgia, in the aftermath of the lynching of Caleb Hill. With equal parts tact and courage, Palfi interviewed and photographed white townspeople by posturing that she sympathized with their situation. Placing these images alongside portraits of the black community, she sought publication for her *There Is No Time: An American Tragedy*. Well ahead of her time, she declared that the photos could only accompany words from Hughes. Three years before Richard Simon suggested this tact for DeCarava's images, Palfi declared: 'the only writer I would permit . . . is Langston Hughes since he has my spirit . . . I feel now either my work appears as I want it to appear or not at all. Then after my death perhaps one will appreciate what I tried to "breathlessly" express when it was very pertinent.'[25]

Including one of her images in his *Pictorial History of the Negro in America* when it came out in 1956, Hughes valued Palfi's photographs. The two became so close that Palfi started referring to Hughes and the Harpers as 'my family' in letters she wrote in 1958, and as late as 1964 her will designated that all her photographs be given to Hughes himself when she died.[26] When Palfi had the chance for a major journalistic breakthrough, it was Hughes she looked to first for guidance. Writing from Greenwood, Mississippi, on 31 March 1963, she tells of missing Hughes twice by phone before writing of her harrowing encounter. On 24 March Palfi witnessed 'gigantic bloodshed' as the local Southern Christian Leadership Conference (SCLC) offices were burned amid shooting that night. She saw into a house where bullets passed over the heads of three babies, and she believed her photographs of it all would be destroyed had she stayed and that 'my testimony' would be lost. Called a 'dirty damn nigger' by a 'policewoman' who also 'tried to smash my camera', Hughes replied that she should have no problems selling her story in Paris, Rome or London.[27] Her documentation of what happened to Robert Moses and Fanny Lou Hamer was published in July as 'Mississippi Malaise' in *Jubilee*, where she included the stunning photo of Annelle

Photographer Marion Palfi would call Hughes her dearest friend for years. Before he died first, she had left all her photographs to Hughes in her will (1947).

Ponder, who looked exhausted and badly shaken as a result of the violent encounter. Because of this coverage, her photos became known to the FBI.[28]

Hughes's friendship with Palfi reminds us of the efforts Hughes invested in other artists as well as his acumen for understanding the visual arts. Well before he so successfully collaborated with DeCarava on *The Sweet Flypaper of Life* in 1955, Hughes had approached Palfi in 1950 with a detailed page-by-page plan for his photo-text of Harlem, *Ups and Downs*.[29] After the two signed a contract, Hughes's idea was rejected by publishers. Had the book appeared in print, *Montage of a Dream Deferred* may have either never been written, or appeared in very different form accompanied by Palfi's photographs. Imagining *Montage* complete with Palfi's photographs is a tantalizing prospect, one that would have most likely amplified the book even more and moved her into the lights of true stardom. For example, Hughes's 'Children's Rhymes' pairs remarkably well with Palfi's most famous image, *In the Shadow of the*

Capitol, Washington, DC, 1946–48, and Hughes had very likely seen this photograph before he wrote the poem.

A friend to Hughes until his death, Palfi contributed images to the 'I Too Am America' exhibit of 1967. Invoking the metaphor Hughes used, Palfi's husband Martin said she was 'not a dreamer, but a fighter with a dream'.[30] A friend to Hughes until his death, Palfi contributed images she took of Native Americans to the exhibit. Palfi supplied an image of seven children at the Henry Street Settlement House in New York City as the first ever cover of *Ebony* in 1945, published *Suffer Little Children* (1952), and was included in Edward Steichen's landmark exhibit 'The Family of Man'. Debuting in early 1955 at New York's MOMA, the 503 artists' prints selected from around the world eventually toured 37 countries over the next eight years. Nine million people saw her work alongside that of Dorothea Lange, Roy DeCarava and Henri Cartier-Bresson. When over four million books of the exhibit sold, Palfi featured with the same number of images that Ansel Adams contributed.

It is Hughes's relationship with Palfi, not DeCarava or Cartier-Bresson, that sparked his imagination while writing *Montage of a Dream Deferred*.[31] In *Montage*, Hughes could not pretend that only the blues came to Harlem. As a result, jazz and bebop collapse distances so that the improvisational nature of jazz stands next to the sublimated violence hidden beneath bebop. In Hughes's mind, bebop was unmistakably intertwined with violence. In his 19 November 1949 newspaper column featuring Jesse Simple, published at the same time Hughes was writing *Montage*, Simple explains that this music 'comes out of them dark days . . . Folks who ain't suffered much cannot play Bop, neither appreciate it.'[32] Boyd is even told that its origins are sounds which are 'beaten right out of some Negro's head'.[33]

In many ways, Hughes's blues poems combine echoes of jazz and bebop to offer something prescient. 'Blues at Dawn' (1951) appears in a sequence that opens with a child waiting to be saved, pimps and whores crying out to God for opposite reasons, blacks passing for white when they have light skin and a soldier too injured to walk. The speaker could be lamenting any of these mistreatments within a traditional twelve-bar blues structure that explains why 'I don't dare remember in the morning.'[34] With enough bad memories to break his head, it seems that only repression allows the speaker to rise out of bed each morning.

'Theme for English B' (1949) quickly became one of Hughes's most anthologized poems. The 22-year-old speaker has just arrived in Harlem from North Carolina, and he is full of dreams similar to those Hughes himself might have had when he entered Columbia University. To fulfill his writing assignment, this speaker argues his essay for class will be 'a part of you, instructor./ You are white –/ yet a part of me, as I am a part of you.'[35] The poem asserts that people must work together side-by-side mirroring what happens between black ink on white paper. Having asked for a page, the instructor is given a poem. Wanting a narrative, he is given the metaphor of a page comprised of black and white, each working together to make meaning. If that can happen on paper, it might also be possible in America. Hughes first published the poem with an image by artist Jacob Lawrence. With its emphasis on 'anatomy', that is, things that are deeper than skin colour, the black-and-white drawing shows a youth brooding over a set of books as he wonders what to write. Based on his work included in *One-way Ticket* (1949), Lawrence would mirror this same style to create six images to accompany Hughes's poems in *Montage* that were never included when the book was published. Lawrence probably backed out in the late stages of the publication process as issues over his compensation from *One-way Ticket* were only resolved when Hughes himself finally paid Lawrence for the money he was due from the publisher.[36] The completed images would have paired with such poems as 'Parade', 'Theme for English B', 'Sliver of

Sermon' and 'Neon Signs'. This reminds us that 'Hughes was probably the most widely and successfully illustrated of modern American poets.'[37]

Anthologized even more, 'Dream Deferred' would soon become Langston Hughes's most popular poem. Originally titled 'Harlem' in 1951, the poem was retitled 'Dream Deferred' by Hughes when included in his final collection in 1967. The original draft of this poem is the only surviving handwritten copy of all the poems Hughes wrote for *Montage*. Hughes immediately knew he had written something special. As such he kept the page and, to document his own assessment, placed a large star with a circle at the top of a very narrow memo page. In many ways, the poem begins where the song 'Strange Fruit' ends. The anti-lynching song made famous by Billie Holiday nears its end by declaring of the lynched body that here is 'fruit for the sun to rot'. Writing with a pencil in his right hand, Hughes begins:

> Does it dry up
> like a raisin
> in the sun?
> Or does it rot

Without crossing it out or starting afresh, Hughes's pencil quickly turned the word 'rot' into 'fester', and then continued with many of the images we know:

> Or does it fester
> like a sore
> and run?

Crossing out the 'and' above and changing it to 'then' kept a rhythm going as Hughes continued to offer similes of food to convey the sensations of what might be lost through delay:

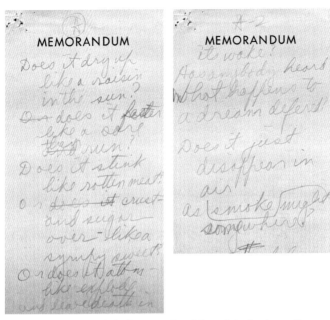

The original handwritten draft of 'Dream Deferred' that ends 'or does it atom-like explode and leave death in its wake?' (August 1948).

Does it stink
like rotten meat?
Or does it crust—
and sugar
over—like a
syrupy sweet?[38]

The idea of 'rot', aborted earlier, returns here. 'Meat' was the type of food most often linked with lynching itself as such atrocities were often referred to derogatorily as 'coon cookings' or 'main fare'.

However, what Hughes writes next is quite shocking to those who know the final poem well. He writes:

Or does it atom-
like explode
and leave death in
its wake?[39]

With the dropping of nuclear weapons on Hiroshima and Nagasaki
a mere three years before Hughes is writing in August 1948, Hughes
brings a destruction from his pencil that carries weight far beyond
the individuals of Harlem. After now asking the question he would
eventually move earlier to begin the poem, 'What happens to/
a dream deferred?', Hughes next offers one more image to extend
the metaphor of nuclear war:

Does it just
disappear in
air
as smoke might
somewhere?[40]

Hughes's pencil drew half circles under 'smoke' and over 'might'
to indicate that the two words should be inverted to eventually
read 'as might smoke somewhere?' What does it mean that the
final italicized image in 'Dream Deferred' that simply reads '*Or
does it explode?*' began as a reference to an atomic bomb?

The reduction to simply 'explode' certainly weights the image
with more ambiguity. In its final version it can allude to rioting,
personal rage, anger and even the sublimated expression of sexual
potency expressed throughout the sequence as a whole. However,
at the very least, Hughes's draft reminds us of the horror that
surrounded everyday life for those living in the wake of the most
devastating days in human history. It also captures the Cold War
tension between capitalism and communism. At its most militant,
it turns suppressed anger in the African American community into

something far more potent than that which dominant culture would term rioting: it envisions black America discharging as a ticking bomb, threatening the very city that Harlem borders. Carried away by weather, the poem asks if this fallout would just disappear with wind. The fear is as much for the world affected and the citizens sacrificed as it is the atom bombs that vanish.

During this period of drafting his most recognizable poem, Hughes had been imagining that what we know as 'Dream Deferred' would be part of a very long sequence titled 'Harlem'. In a later draft, Hughes did something else very interesting. Above where his pencil has circled endlessly over the already crossed-through 'atom-like', he writes out 'syrupy' in the margin, to be sure his hand agrees with his eyes that it is being spelled correctly. Then, Hughes adds a new line to rhyme with his more ambiguous 'explode': 'Maybe it just sags/ like a heavy load.' One possibility for the source of this imagery comes from considering another contemporaneous project. Hughes was simultaneously revising his opera *Troubled Island*, where characters speak of a 'heavy load' on three occasions. On each occasion the imagery references fruit, adding one more potential connection between this poem and lynching.[41]

Hughes's poem was vaulted into greatest notoriety when Lorraine Hansberry took the first image of Hughes's poem as the final title of her 1959 play *A Raisin in the Sun*. When Hansberry graciously wrote to Hughes for his permission to use the title, the poet didn't even consider asking for royalties.[42] With the change in title, audiences and critics would be drawn to the explosions of Walter Lee, the heartbreak of losing unborn children and Mama's lonely plant even more than they would notice the example Mama sets for her son as she is never too weary to climb the stairs with her arms full of groceries. Hughes's actual role in the play's success was muted, but he beamed for having 'discovered' Claudia McNeil when she starred earlier in his *Simply Heavenly* (1957). Now playing Mama in *Raisin*, Hughes sent her flowers on opening night, which she acknowledged before bemoaning how he 'disappeared so fast into the crowd I didn't get a chance to make another dinner date'.[43] McNeil would become so well known she would soon start appearing in her own adverts selling Reinhart Beer and Hughes would read from friends that she had apparently changed as a result of her success to become 'a victim of a dream fulfilled'.[44] The success of the play would even alter the way Hughes named his own poem. In April 1960, preparing for a radio interview in Chapel Hill, North Carolina, Hughes made a handwritten list of poems he wanted to share on air and one line read merely: 'Raisin in the Sun'.[45]

The impact of Hansberry's play on Hughes and his poetry was immense. Printed in every programme for the play's 538 consecutive appearances on Broadway, every audience member saw the poem, and perhaps even thought the play had simply dramatized Hughes's own themes. Moreover, by the end of the year it was Hughes (not Hansberry) who was posing for Smirnoff Vodka adverts in *Ebony*. Within only three weeks of the play's immediate success (and subsequent breakthrough Hollywood film contact), Martin Luther King Jr took notice of Langston Hughes's poem and first began speaking about 'Shattered Dreams and Blasted Hopes'. He took the perspective of unfulfilled dreams into his repertoire long before his dream became optimistic and uplifting.[46]

'Dream Deferred' has continued to surface in countless key political and cultural moments ever since it was published. One such moment came when Barack Obama accepted his party's nomination for president of the United States at the Democratic National Convention held in Denver, Colorado, on 28 August 2008. Candidate Obama's speech was carefully planned for just this calendar date as it was 45 years to the day that Martin Luther King Jr delivered the most recognizable version of his 'I Have a Dream' speech in Washington, DC. In the midst of telling his audience what King's listeners heard in 1963, Obama noted those demonstrators 'could have heard many things. They could have heard words of anger and discord, they could have been told to succumb to the fears and frustrations of so many dreams deferred'.[47]

On the evening when the Democratic Party nominated the first African American presidential candidate in American history, Obama's reference to Hughes's 'Dream Deferred' cast the poet as an unfortunate adversary to hope and change. It appeared that his ideas were the ones that bemoaned fate rather than inspired and exhorted listeners to action.[48] The irony was that when Obama thought he was merely alluding to King later in his speech, he was actually activating ideas from Hughes's poem 'Mother to Son' as they had become internalized by King himself. Listeners heard: 'we cannot walk alone, the preacher cried, and as we walk we must make the pledge that we shall always march ahead. We cannot turn back, America, we cannot turn back.' Like Obama himself, the audience had no idea that King's words were ones the preacher learned from sampling 'Mother to Son' when the 1955 Montgomery Bus Boycott forced black women to struggle without public transportation and serve as exemplary models to their children.[49] Langston Hughes was reviled as a subversive in political campaigns through the early twenty-first century, and it would not be until social media's circulation of Hughes's poem 'Kids Who Die' (1938) in the wake of Trayvon Martin's murder in 2012 that it became safe for politicians such as President Obama to invoke his name.

9

Seeing Red, 1953–60

On 21 March 1953, Hughes received a subpoena: 'YOU ARE
HEREBY COMMANDED to appear before the SENATE PERMANENT
SUB committee on INVESTIGATIONS of the Senate of the United
States. HEREOF FAIL NOT, as you will answer your default under
. . . pains and penalties.'[1] As if the shear formality of the invitation
were not overwhelming enough, Hughes knew that the man he
was being asked to face was none other than the infamous Joseph
McCarthy. With just two days to try and arrange his travels, attorney
William Lloyd Garrison won his client one extra day to arrive in
Washington, DC, on Tuesday 24 March.[2] While this was not the
more recognized House Un-American Activities Committee (HUAC),
a committee he had joined playwright Arthur Miller in speaking
out against publicly three years earlier when two members of the
Hollywood Ten were jailed for 'taking the fifth', the name of the
committee made no difference to Hughes or history. Understanding
nothing of McCarthy's complex motivations, Hughes assumed he
was being called to answer for his subversive activities and to name
names of those he knew to be members of the Communist Party.
The stakes were clearly as high as they could be: two years earlier
his editor Max Lieber, a card-carrying member of the Communist
Party, had fled to Mexico when called to testify.[3]

Though he never uncovered a single communist during his
career, McCarthy's official impetus for calling Hughes to testify was
the hyper-concern that America was not being portrayed favourably

in the books housed overseas in U.S. Information Centers. Though neither McCarthy nor his accomplice Roy Cohn had yet set foot in any of these libraries, they claimed that 51 centres included sixteen of Hughes's books. This was not true: only two of Hughes's tamest books, *Not Without Laughter* (1930) and *Fields of Wonder* (1947), were in (and subsequently removed) from these centres. Unaware of this, Hughes had come to fight and 'stood his ground' when he met privately in executive session with Cohn and Senator Everett Dirksen.[4] However, Hughes had come 'armed for the wrong fight'.[5] Though he 'defended himself tenaciously', it was not enough to dissuade 'McCarthy and Cohn from resuming the interrogation in public'.[6]

It would only be understood half a century later from studying the patterns and results of these private sessions that 'witnesses who stood up to McCarthy in closed session, and did so articulately, tended not to get called up into the public session.'[7] With McCarthy not attending the executive session, Hughes was assessed by Cohn, who must have been given at least some pause when Hughes offered what seemed to be his entire personal history of experiencing racism in America. Hughes's response was so exhaustive, and clever, that he was interrupted by an exasperated Cohn. At that point, Hughes had only covered the first nineteen years of his life in what was 'a monologue unparalleled in the records of the McCarthy Committee for its unbroken duration'.[8] When Cohn asked about the poems 'One More "S" in the U.S.A.' and 'Goodbye Christ', Hughes had no way of knowing that the majority of the committee's evidence was built on the FBI's scant collection of news items collected under the guise of investigation.

One hour into the first interrogation, Roy Cohn exploded in response to Hughes's elusiveness. Asked if he ever desired a Soviet form of government in America, Hughes replied: 'Would you permit me to think about it?'[9] Hughes refused to name names of known communists, and for some reason Senator Dirksen called for a recess as Hughes had moved passed his earlier 'filibustering' and was now becoming more 'selectively adamant'.[10]

On 25 March Hughes and his first attorney Frank Reeves met with McCarthy to negotiate the parameters of his public testimony. It is possible that Hughes also had another meeting that day as well with Cohn and David Schine, a hotel owner of some influence serving as chief consultant of the committee.[11] While the threat of perjury charges may or may not have hung latent in the air, it appears that Hughes had two stipulations for this formal appearance, and each of these represented duel motivations. First, to protect any remaining prospects of a successful lecture career, Hughes did not want McCarthy to read lines from 'Goodbye Christ' on television. This was granted, and McCarthy smoothly asked at the end of the testimony that the poem be entered silently into the written record. Second, demonstrating his own ethics and consciousness, Hughes would not be asked to name names. Though it was not this committee's goal, Hughes's executive session reveals that he had unequivocally decided that he would not provide any names.

With the parameters in place, Hughes's official televised testimony on 26 March was as scripted as any daytime soap opera. The visuals were not good for Hughes. Now his moustache was half the length of his lip, too similar to Hitler's, even though Hughes wore his three times as thin. Years later it would be suggested that McCarthy saw attacking African Americans as 'bullying and therefore bad politics', so McCarthy was surely pleased to maintain a sense of decorum and not hedge on his word.[12] In fact, unbeknownst to Hughes or anyone else McCarthy called before the committee, the script was exactly what the committee was looking for in trying to achieve its covert goal of showing that the State Department had a small pool of subversives who were secretly sliding books into overseas libraries that were either pro-communist or at least un-American. McCarthy wanted to build a case allowing him to go after reds within the government,

With both radio and television broadcasting live, Hughes testifies in Washington, DC, before the McCarthy Committee on 26 March 1953 while attorney Frank Reeves sits by his side.

not authors like Hughes. As David Chinitz has so aptly shown, when Hughes showed his past leftist leanings, repudiated that stance and, most importantly, appeared shocked that his revolutionary books were in such information centres, McCarthy had exactly what he wanted: another author who could be used to build an ever stronger case for purging people from the State Department on suspicions of colluding with Russia's meddling. In the end, neither naming names nor skewering authors who were presently communists were the true aims of this very elaborate game.[13]

Hughes had come prepared to score one very potent strike against McCarthy. Before travelling to Washington, DC, Hughes had typed up a statement dated 23 March that he was planning to read at his formal hearing. He ended by summarizing his world view. Appearing to only be speaking of Haitian history, he referenced his recent opera *Troubled Island*. Though it was also his signature poem, Hughes coyly referenced it as an aria that 'expresses my own personal feelings in regard to social and political relations'.[14] He then typed the full text of 'I Dream a World' (1945). Hughes thought to supply a rhetorical move based on the opera that would have linked McCarthy to the corrupt Dessalines, and Hughes himself to the sage Martel. Hughes did this by placing extra emphasis on the word 'share' when he wrote: 'A world I dream where black or white,/ Whatever race you be,/ Will *share* the bounties of the earth.' It is no coincidence that the only other version of this poem in Hughes's file in which 'share' is also emphasized this way bears these typed words in the lower right-hand corner: 'Martel's aria from *Troubled Island* an Opera with over-tones for today'.[15] This emphasis amplified the socialist conditions in which the poem was created in 1936 and Hughes's continued anti-capitalist stand against 'greed' and 'avarice'.[16] Knowing Hughes intended to, but never did, share his socialist and un-American vision with McCarthy simultaneously reveals how prepared Hughes was to argue when he left New York, and just how much he, for whatever reasons, capitulated in Washington.

The final act of this interrogation had overtones that Hughes would never understand. As if to assure his witness who had won, there was no mistake when McCarthy winked at Hughes after he was excused.[17] More confusing to the poet, he recalled that Cohn said to him that J. Edgar Hoover had once used 'Goodbye Christ' in a speech of his. Through open communication between the FBI and McCarthy, Cohn was signalling that Hughes had come fully into the FBI's sights when he refused to allow 'Goodbye Christ' to be published in a collection that included Hoover's speech. In fact, the entire ramping up of surveillance and harassment against the writer certainly appears to stem directly from the feud over this publication. This connection was one Hughes never realized. In the end, Hoover's personal vindictiveness over the actual issue of publication itself went so far as to be the most likely reason copies of Hughes's *Simple Speaks His Mind* were sabotaged three years earlier, keeping what was destined to be a bestseller from earning that distinguished moniker.[18]

The backdraft from this event has always struck readers very differently. Suggesting that Hughes had rhetorically disarmed his inquisitors, Arnold Rampersad declared that Hughes's public testimony is a 'tour de force'.[19] Several other emerging scholars have agreed. However, Faith Berry, remembering that other options were available to Hughes, such as refusing to testify as Arthur Miller would or being as openly defiant as Paul Robeson, suggested that Hughes disappointed many of those on the left in what appeared to be moments where he was 'pulverized into submission' and ended this skewing when 'the capitulation was complete'.[20] Decades later, David Chinitz would declare that what 'Hughes had feared would deal his career a deathblow, had instead became the instrument of his vindication. The committee had, in effect, pronounced Hughes a reformed communist and given him the ammunition to defend himself from future harassment.'[21] The harassments Hughes received varied greatly. On the one hand, Hughes wrote with relieved delight to his attorney Frank Reeves two weeks after the event that without his legal counsel he 'would have been a lost ball in the high weeds'. Moreover, his gratitude continued as he declared that the results of the 'open hearing' (what he calls a 'TV show') were that 'all my publishers are going ahead with their publishing plans in relation to my work.'[22]

On the other hand, Hughes had never really made much money from royalties. Rather it was his speaking engagements that often sustained the bulk of his income. Unlike Miller or Robeson, Hughes could not afford the luxury of removing himself entirely from such appearances. He had already felt the effect of earlier controversies, and future ones had to be avoided not on moral grounds but financial ones. When his lecture bureau Colston Leigh 'dropped him like a hot potato' after representing him since 1946, any vindication must have felt like trying to live on tomorrow's bread. Worse, Hughes's trip to the capital did nothing to dissuade former Communist Party member Manning Johnson from flatly declaring

Hughes gathered children to plant a flower garden outside his Harlem stoop, where every child's name appeared on a sign planted nearby, *c.* 1955.

before the HUAC only two months later that Hughes was indeed a communist.[23] In some regards, Hughes must have felt relieved that things were not worse. He had somehow simultaneously acquitted himself well or let people down depending upon the individual politics of every friend. Only one year later Edwin R. Murrow would expose McCarthy's witch hunts, and the senator died in a cloud of ridicule three years after Hughes's public testimony in 1957.

The results are clear. Hughes's testimony had not cleared him of any suspicions. In fact, the FBI maintained its file until its last entry in 1965. Moreover, his appearance and testimony 'did not end hostility from the right', a torment that would hound him even beyond the grave.[24] Though Hughes worked to try and use the testimony as the means to clear the air once and for all, he also 'played it safe' by turning in even greater measure to write five 'first' books, knowing literature for children was always patriotic. He also ramped up his efforts as an editor, knowing the actual works collected in his volumes were not written under his name. Finally, he always had his alter ego Simple, projecting his sentiments into arguments where it could be hard to decipher the author's stance on current issues. Being 'red' was a virus, and Hughes had to be careful not to infect those with whom he came into contact. As to the scholarly implications, Cary Nelson is not alone in believing that for years our 'restricted and depolarized canon of modernism' has been impacted by 'our discipline's testimony before HUAC'.[25]

As natural extensions of Hughes's personality, he gladly took on these editorial tasks, even turning down the chance at this time for other projects such as serving as the Ghanaian prime minister Kwame Nkrumah's official biographer.[26] A man who was very much in tune with children, the poet became even more famous in his neighbourhood for establishing a small garden in the front of his Harlem home. In about 1954 he taught children how plants grow by having each participant place a stake with their name near the aster or marigold they had planted and then tended. The sign in the garden appeared as a large lollipop to welcome children. When Hughes was not writing books for children, he was editing others. His *Famous Negro Music Makers* (1955), *A Pictorial History of the Negro in America*, with Milton Meltzer (1956), and *Famous Negro Heroes of America* (1958) allowed him to expand much of the same research he used in the 'first' books series and pitch his editorial voice for an adult audience.

The horrific lynching of Emmett Till was one of the biggest news stories of 1955. Hughes's poetic response, 'Mississippi–1955', appeared in print about two weeks after the event. What was clear to readers of the newspapers in which Hughes's poem appeared, including the 1 October edition of his *Chicago Defender*, has lost the immediate context of the event itself to leave readers of 'Mississippi–1955' uncertain about Till's role in inspiring the poem. We now know that Hughes not only responded, but was the first African American poet of note to address the event in verse.[27] Hughes's choice to eventually remove any dedication to Till, or to reference him specifically in its republished lines, has resulted in significant confusion about how to read this important poem.

Inspired to change a world where Emmett Till could be lynched and the murderers set free, the Montgomery Bus Boycott came under Hughes's lens immediately after Rosa Parks was arrested in December 1955. Inspired by her time at Highlander Folk School, and remarkably clear about every detail for what would make for a legal refusal to move from her bus seat, Parks and E. D. Nixon thrust a recently arrived pastor into heading a protest expected to last no more than a week. When Martin Luther King Jr accepted what he expected to be nothing more than a figurehead role as leader of the newly formed Montgomery Improvement Association, he was not only avoiding a split between the city's two more established rival pastors, he was stepping onto a path that would change the course of American history.

King's presence so deeply impacted Hughes that the preacher became an integral part of both his journalism and poetry. Beginning in 1956, King would appear as the subject or earn a key mention in no less than forty articles Hughes wrote for the *Chicago Defender*. On two occasions in 1957 Hughes declared that King would become a 'permanent fixture of black history'.[28] Often allowing Simple to figuratively travel, Hughes devoted an entire article to King in 1957 where he offered satirical commentary on the first Prayer Pilgrimage held in Washington, DC. Attending himself, Hughes suggested King would have been the best person to deliver the final prayer because he would not have to 'read no prayer off no paper'.[29] On other occasions he imagined King running for president, and later explained that Simple's lack of self-control would push him beyond non-violence were he to attend the famous march from Selma in 1965.[30]

King would make numerous appearances in Hughes's works. When Hughes penned the play *The Ballot and Me* (1956) to support a voter registration drive in Harlem, he ended his play with an idea King used in his first major national address before a NAACP convention in San Francisco.[31] The two missed a chance to meet there as the poet chose not to attend.[32] King's address was republished in *u.s. News and World Report*, where Hughes probably read the ending to King's speech. This ending followed his own poem 'Mother to Son', which appeared in its entirety in the speech directly before King's final words, which Hughes then referenced word for word in his 1956 play: 'If you can't fly, run; if you can't run, walk; if you can't walk, crawl, but by all means keep moving!'[33]

Moreover, Hughes was the first person King thought of when it was time to write his first book as he approached Hughes about collaborating on what came to be *Stride to Freedom: The Montgomery Story* (1958).[34] Accepting so many projects, it is uncertain if his decision to respectfully decline telling the story of the bus boycott in prose was based on being overwhelmed, or apprehension (based on experience) about collaborating. It may also show Hughes being careful about bringing his radical past to bear on a movement that would be accused of being infiltrated by communists. Siding with the Southern Christian Leadership Conference (SCLC) could also have tested his long-standing relationships with both Adam Clayton Powell and the NAACP.

Hughes's first poetic response to King came during the tension of the bus boycott when he published 'Brotherly Love' on 18 August 1956. He later made revisions, and published it in his own newspaper column on 23 March 1957. He ended his prose with Simple's typical humour counter-balancing the more formally educated Boyd: 'There are plenty of Jim Crowers who speak fine grammar, but do very evil . . . I figure it is better to do right than to write right.'[35] Both early versions of the published poem are more hostile than they appeared in future printings as part of Hughes's subtitle was inadvertently omitted by later editors. When it appeared in *The Nation*, Hughes originally subtitled 'Brotherly Love' with 'A Little Letter to the White

Citizens Councils of the South'. The omission of 'Councils' in subsequent editions removes the historical reality of these white supremacist hate groups and the behaviour that Simple was directly challenging.

Expecting King to accept an award where Hughes was keynote speaker, the poem benefitted from four additional drafts that Hughes made to prepare for his address to the Windy City Press Club in Chicago. Before the 10 January 1957 event, Hughes considered new endings and made it especially clear in his introductory comments that the poem is spoken by Simple himself, making it one of the rare places where the prose character can be heard fluently in Hughes's verses.

Hughes's actual speech before the public reading of the poem communicated his deep and abiding passion for the news. Speaking to journalists formally, Hughes would have much rather talked on the pavement where his cigarette could flutter as if his lips had wings. Instead, here his sing-song voice went bouncing through typed pages as he read through his wide black-rimmed glasses. He made it clear how much he admired newspapers, and his comments were both humorous and sincere:

I have been exposed to lots of literature in my time – but my favorite reading is the Negro press. Perhaps it should be the *Iliad*, the *Odyssey*, Shakespeare, or Tolstoy, but it isn't. It is the Negro press. Every week the Lord sends, if possible, in Harlem I buy the AFRO, the COURIER, the AMSTERDAM NEWS, the AGE, and, of course, the DEFENDER for which I write – so I can read myself. Also I buy whatever local colored papers there are in whatever city I may be when traveling. Whenever I find myself in a town where the colored papers are not available – like Carmel, California, for instance – I feel on week-ends as though I were completely out of this world and have lost contact with my people. Abroad the two things I miss most are American ice cream and Negro papers.[36]

Hughes also added that 'Humor is a weapon, too', before arguing for his larger point, which can also be read as a defence of Simple himself: 'Since we have not been able to moralize our enemies out of existence with indignant editorials, maybe we could laugh them to death with well-aimed ridicule.'[37] Hughes would always be inspired to read and write the news, and the appearance of 'Rev. King', as his articles most frequently named him, led him into some imaginative possibilities. When Simple dreamed in a May 1963 article that he himself was president of the United States, his first order of business was to declare 'I hereby command the misusers to turn over all dogs, prod rods, and fire hoses to Rev. Martin Luther King.'[38]

Hughes had struggled to start his second autobiography eleven years earlier, but he picked up the task in earnest in 1954. It would not be until May 1955 and the subsequent autumn of the same year that Hughes would revisit his time covering Spain's civil war and trip to the USSR. Covering the years of 1931–8 offered a particular challenge in how to address his heightened radicalism throughout the decade. Though it was an autobiography, Hughes guarded such privacy as carefully as always. In autumn 1956 Hughes attended the 'biggest book party', and it was shared with releases by lawyer Pauli Murray, former boxer Henry Armstrong and Eartha Kitt, who was 'at the height of her stardom'.[39] While his simultaneous publication work as an editor with Milton Meltzer of *A Pictorial History of the Negro in America* heralded praise, successfully staying in print for the next 25 years, Hughes's autobiography initially challenged readers' own beliefs and feelings about the Soviet Union. To most, he was even-handed in assessing the country's absence of racism and abject poverty, but his friends from the left were again puzzled by omissions of his own radical activism. (These omissions were also not to be found anywhere in the 22 chapters Hughes drafted but did not publish.)

One friend from Carmel, California, Maria Short, may have summed up Hughes's choices best with regard to leaving out references to the John Reed Club and his other involvements: 'you are a wise person' and 'I am not'.[40] However, Hughes always knew the importance of context and audience. Only weeks after its publication, Hughes addressed the racism Autherine Lucy faced trying to integrate the South in a *Chicago Defender* column: 'If Miss Lucy wanted to go to bed with a white man instead of to college with one, nobody at the University of Alabama would throw stones at her, nor defy the Supreme Court.'[41]

With the poetry-to-jazz movement capturing the hearts of 'beats' in Greenwich Village, Hughes revived a practice he had started himself over thirty years earlier in 1926. Hughes performed on many Sunday evenings in the late 1950s with the culmination coming when he recorded his onstage collaboration with bassist Charles Mingus in the spring of 1958. Not a gifted reader, the excitement of the music sometimes overwhelmed the moment, such as when a drum roll and crashing cymbals punctuate '*or does it explode*' at the end of 'Dream Deferred'. However, the tempos that create the rhythms for many of Hughes's verses remind all listeners just how hip Hughes could be. And while the arrival of *The Langston Hughes Reader* that same year stunned its author for the range of subject-matter covered in its five hundred pages, it was Knopf's *Selected Poems* that excited Hughes more. Where the *Reader* offered a selection of his short stories, translations, song lyrics, two plays, speeches, extensive excerpts from his novels and two autobiographies, it was the *Selected Poems* that Hughes was hanging high hopes on when it appeared on 23 March 1959, a mere twelve days after the New York premiere of the play *A Raisin in the Sun*. In the short run, he would not be disappointed.

The poet's excitement in having his poems collected buoyed optimism that his prestige would grow. Hughes had one honour in mind that had eluded him when he wrote directly to his good friend Arna Bontemps: 'I send you under separate cover Knopf's Spring Catalogue marketing my *Selected Poems* so you might send

it to the Spingarn Award Selection Committee if you deem it now
the moment to make that nomination.'[42] Hughes would win the
award in 1960, following Duke Ellington, Jackie Robinson and
Martin Luther King Jr as past winners. However, the poems Hughes
left on the editing floor reveal that what Hughes had offered to
represent himself at this time in his career was a very sanitized
image. Most telling, when Hughes had seven blank pages to fill,
he wrote tame poems about 'tambourines' while simultaneously
republishing volatile works such as 'Not for Publication' overseas
in Nigeria.[43] Hughes did not want to announce in *Selected Poems*
that, were Christ to return to America today, he would be barred
from church for being too radical. Any black man who said such
things, 'may be crucified'.[44]

When it came to representing his response to the lynching of
Emmett Till, neither of the two distinct poems he devoted to the
event were to be found in his *Selected Poems*. Moreover, poems such
as 'Brotherly Love' were left out, as if Hughes were an apolitical poet.
In fact, Hughes appears to have instead taken a covert approach on
at least one occasion to simultaneously address and veil his social
concerns. When the poem that came to be known as 'Negro' was
first published in 1922 as 'Proem', it referenced the practice of
violence Hughes knew well by stating 'They lynch me now in
Texas.'[45] However, he altered this line when it appeared in 1959.

Hughes's preparations for a poetry-to-jazz event in early 1959
capture part of his thought process in making this revision. As
he prepared to play with the Tony Stroll Trio, perhaps to raise
money for Karamu House in Cleveland, Hughes imagined the
poem performed along with the songs 'Blue Sands' or 'Caravan',
writing the first title in red, and the second in pencil.[46] His pencil
also underlines the word 'Africa' in the third line of the poem to
suggest he thought 'Blue Sands' a better fit for the introduction.
Noting a 'low drum roll into big boom' at this exact line, he revises
the line in pencil to read: 'They bomb me now in Alabama.' Perhaps

written during a rehearsal, Hughes adds a red 'STOP' just before this line to signal where the music will build to this explosion on the word 'bomb'. However, held to the light, it is clear that the line that Hughes is crossing out for revision had actually been typed: 'They mob me in Texas.'[47]

While he followed this poem with 'Africa' immediately after, with a flute playing 'tacit', Hughes makes two final choices. First, he chooses 'Caravan' as the song over 'Blue Sands'. More interesting, he offers yet another line about violence in the same space, and this one changes in a very significant way one final time again before publication as he settles on: 'They lynch me still in Mississippi.'[48] Hughes avoided overtly saying: 'They lynched Emmett Till in Mississippi.' This subtle alteration 'slyly embeds Till's name', something easily heard by repeating each variant.[49] The parallels between 'lynch me still' and 'lynch Emmett Till' seem to reveal both Hughes's ability and desire to be covert in this edition.

The ramifications of Hughes's editorial choices may have been a combination of the pressures he felt to move away from radicalism as well as his desire to reach the broadest possible audience in what he rightly hoped would bring him award-winning recognition. By 1961 Hughes seems to have realized this when he mused to his friend 'My *Selected Poems* (of a sort), just came out in Italy.'[50] Hughes's next gesture hints at how much his appearance before McCarthy wounded him as he suggests that this book could be considered for inclusion in one of the U.S. Information Centers. The barb is not lost on his reader, who coyly suggests that their friend Carl Rowan look into including formally omitted black authors such as Hughes.[51] The very subject of Hughes's Senate testimony in 1953 is both the tongue-in-cheek jest and very real context that made such a conservative approach to the book's contents necessary.

The impact of *Selected Poems* in shaping Hughes's persona cannot be overstated. In fact, with *The Collected Poems of Langston Hughes* not available until 1994, *Selected Poems* stood as the de facto complete poems of Hughes for no less than 35 years. As such, scholars, students and writers wanting a comprehensive volume on Hughes's poetry during this era turned to the 1959 edition, allowing it to shape their perceptions. Subjects such as his socialist poems and nearly three dozen responses to lynching were not found in its pages. It is revealing that when Elizabeth Alexander turned to praise the poet who put African Americans into the canon, she imagined all her readers had experienced later editions of this volume well into the early 1990s. She referred to the later cover images featuring a smiling Hughes tapping away on his typewriter with matches resting on an unsmoked pack of Camel cigarettes in the background.[52] Republished so often it has been forgotten that the original 1959 version instead featured an image taken by Henri Cartier-Bresson of an older Hughes standing in his Harlem studio in a striped button-down shirt, where the black-and-white film masked the yellow colour of his crooked teeth. He was not pretending to write at all, turning his back on the Underwood Standard typewriter on his desk. There were two additional possessions he kept until he died. He stood for that image while the large ring on his right hand hung just below the camera's frame, and Elsie Roxborough's photograph sat out of reach high upon his window bookcase in the corner. Due to the ultraconservative era, he would almost seem to become younger every year in the minds of readers who seemed to always picture him in his twenties, so that he was only the leading figure of the New Negro Movement.

10

Bright Tomorrows, 1960–62

Langston Hughes would never be more popular than he was in 1960. He had just won the NAACP's highest honour, joining the likes of Jackie Robinson, Duke Ellington and Martin Luther King Jr as winner of the Spingarn medal. Hughes's *Selected Poems* was now available, providing the first collected verse spanning his entire career. A line from one of his poems was the title of Broadway's hottest play, as *A Raisin in the Sun* was still enjoying unparalleled success. Some critics would oversimplify the play's theme of 'shattered dreams' as a mere dramatization of his own poem 'Dream Deferred'.[1] In many classrooms, the play is actually taught that way.[2] The play's success would eclipse his own *Mulatto* for the longest-running play by an African American. All this attention led Smirnoff Vodka to feature Hughes in an advertising campaign where his full-page photo ran in *Ebony* magazine. With a subscription of more than 650,000, and many more reading it in doctors' offices and beauty salons, the suave Hughes is identified in the caption as a 'famous poet, lyric writer, lecturer and critic' who asked 'Why settle for anything less than the vodka of vodkas?' The advert shows how recognizable Langston Hughes was by 1960.

Hughes's high profile had resulted in numerous invitations. At the very end of 1959 Hughes immediately responded to a letter in which he read: 'This will be a somewhat unusual request.' Sunday 24 January was to feature a Salute to A. Philip Randolph. Free and open to the

Hughes would never be more popular than he was in 1960. Here he appears in an advertisement for Smirnoff Vodka described as a 'famous poet, lyric writer, lecturer and critic'.

public at Carnegie Hall, the writer queried whether Hughes would write a poem in honour of Mr Randolph because 'A poetic tribute by our greatest poet and America's best to one of our purest leaders is a matchless combination.' The letter ended with these words:

To add a personal note – my admiration for your works is not only expressed in my personal conversations, but I can no longer count the numbers of times and places, all over the nation, in my addresses and sermons in which I have read your poems. I know of no better way to express in beauty the heartbeat and struggle of our people.

I hope you can find it possible to fulfill this request.

With warmest personal regards,

Very sincerely,

Martin Luther King, Jr.[3]

Despite an ever-growing list of obligations, the blue signature above the name must have made an immediate impact on Hughes, and he delivered his poem directly to King with the title 'Poem for a Man'. Knowing King read and used his poetry, Hughes later sent copies of 'Merry-Go-Round', ideal for a man who had led a bus boycott, and an unpublished piece of stitched-together clichés titled 'Prayer for the Mantle Piece', apparently trying to show King his spiritual side.

Uncertain about the controversy that an in-person appearance might bring to the occasion, and now well aware of the impact surrounding the reverend's suspected subversive leanings, Hughes hid out in room 2428 of the Waldorf Towers during the event. He met Hugh Woodings there at 4.30 p.m., while leading lady of *A Raisin in the Sun*, Ruby Dee, performed the poem at the celebration.[4] He was wise to do so. Despite his popularity in the black community, Hughes's forthcoming reading tour would be met with bomb threats and cancelled events. The erroneous reports published by both *Time* magazine and the *New York Times* earlier in the year asserting Hughes had dined in Harlem with Fidel Castro (accompanied by poet Allen Ginsberg) had outraged even close friends and fuelled the flames of those already suspicious. Thus, instead of heading out to a crowd, Hughes sent the radiant star of *A Raisin in the Sun* an early morning wire the next day exclaiming:

'Thank you so very much for what friends in attendance at Randolph Testimonial tell me was your beautiful rendition of my poem last night. Sorry I had to miss it.'[5]

While drafting another poem during this time, Hughes directly noted King's Southern Christian Leadership Conference (SCLC) when he wrote that the 'REDS' being investigated included everyone from 'CASTRO' and 'NKRUMAH' to 'THE RADICALS IN THAT/ SOUTHERN CONFERENCE'.[6] Given his numerous phone conversations with Bayard Rustin, just severed from serving in the SCLC, Hughes probably heard this news not from the papers but directly from men such as Rustin, who were so affected by smear campaigns that they ended up actually losing professional positions. We can only imagine the subjects and tact expressed in the many carefully logged phone conversations between the two men. When they spoke on 10 June 1960, Rustin must have mentioned the resignation he was about to submit to King two weeks later. This took place a mere month before Hughes started drafting the above poem, but everything was spoken as neither exchanged written letters preserved for our posterity.[7]

Rustin's resignation from the SCLC may have had a profound effect on Hughes. As Dr King planned a protest against the Democratic Convention in Los Angeles to move civil rights reform to the forefront, Harlem's very own congressman Adam Clayton Powell Jr blackmailed King. If the picketing was not called off, Powell was threatening to spread the false rumour that the former communist and currently closeted homosexual Rustin was having an affair with King. If not merely bullying a rival, Powell may have feared such protests would keep him from being named to important committees within his own party. Unfounded, the outlandish threat resulted in Rustin stepping away from the SCLC in June. In fact, even at the end of the year, the odour surrounding Rustin had not dissipated, as he had to remove himself from a speaking engagement in October when the AFL-CIO, the largest federation of unions in the u.s., asserted they would not donate funds to the sNCC-sponsored event if he remained on the programme. Rustin would remain painfully distanced from the civil rights movement for the next three and a half years.[8]

Along with the earlier dismissal in the spring of no less than a dozen Alabama State faculty, friends of King fired for their suspected communist beliefs, Hughes had several reasons to keep more than arm's length away from the fray. Proximity demanded some heartfelt allegiance to Powell for what he meant to Harlem. In fact, Hughes had even written a campaign jingle in the past to support Powell.[9] Fortunately Hughes's own sexuality had remained an unknowable position so that his own choices could not be used by others as a weapon against him. Past publication support in *The Crisis* also directed his admiration to Roy Wilkins and the NAACP, while King's use of his own poetry and clear star power could not be ignored. There were as many factions within the civil rights movement as there are denominations in the Christian Church. Trying to keep everyone happy, this lack of homogeneity in the black fight for freedom subsequently tore Hughes in many directions even as his red past and carefully concealed bisexuality were clear liabilities. Worse, as Rustin himself felt, such attention could distract from the larger cause of civil rights itself.

As one of only a select number of black preachers at the time to hold a PhD, King had found that invoking Hughes had connected with audiences to remind listeners that he was still a man of the people. King recited 'Mother to Son' from memory to his congregation in May 1956 while his wife Coretta sat in the pews, celebrating her first Mother's Day as a parent. He invoked the dark and light imagery of 'Youth' in more than seventy different places, including letters, addresses and prayers.[10] At the same time, in the speech that scholars would recognize as the roots of his own famous dream, King had rewritten lines of 'I Dream a World', focusing on the connectivity of the biblical and socialist idea of a new world before eventually (and directly) invoking Hughes's dream imagery on numerous occasions.[11]

The connections between these two icons demonstrate how Hughes's poetry played as much of a key role in the civil rights movement as it did in shaping the New Negro Movement. King had become the subject of Hughes's poem 'Brotherly Love' in August 1956, and King responded by reworking one of its lines to form the dramatic ending used in several of his civil rights speeches.[12] More recently, King had seized upon the success of *A Raisin in the Sun* itself to bring together integrated audiences when he delivered his sermon 'Shattered Dreams' a mere three weeks after the play's debut.[13] Hughes would continue to inform the language of King throughout the remainder of the leader's lifetime, and 'Let America Be America Again' is referenced specifically in King's famous 4 April 1967 'Beyond Vietnam' speech, where the preacher was among the very first to anticipate what would eventually become widespread disdain for American involvement in the Vietnam War.[14]

Hughes's poetry had long centred on dreams, and the preacher riffed on this theme numerous times. After directly engaging with poems about dreams such as 'I Dream a World', 'Poem for a Man' and 'Dream Deferred', King's famous 'I Have a Dream' speech at the March on Washington riffed on Hughes's dream imagery by weaving it together with cultural ideas of the American Dream and Christianity's visions of prophecy. Martin Luther King Jr became the star performer of some of Langston Hughes's greatest scripts. Moreover, King inspired Hughes, making key appearances in many of his own works.[15]

Just as 1959 had ended with Hughes in direct contact with King, the two men would usher in the new Kennedy era by travelling together to Nigeria to celebrate Governor Nnamdi Azikiwe's inauguration as the first native governor general. As leader of the country just freed from the colonial hands of the English, Azikiwe mimicked King himself when he ended the most important speech of his career by reading Hughes's 'Youth' in its entirety as the final lines he delivered at his own inauguration. Just after hearing Azikiwe recite it, King returned to the poem immediately, where he began citing it more accurately than he had in the years before, when he often improvised its lines for his own purposes.[16]

Hughes's relationship with Africa took on great significance in the 1960s. As a man who owned several newspapers throughout the region, Azikiwe had brought Hughes a broad readership by publishing his poems in places such as the *West African Pilot* for years. In fact, Hughes had received letters from more than a hundred Nigerians who loved seeing his poetry in print in their native land. Hughes even revised a poem from 1942 originally about Gandhi and made 'Zik in Jail' about the new leader.[17] Hughes soon demonstrated remarkable foresight by editing two volumes in which he recognized Africa's great literary tradition long before others in the Americas. His *First Book of Africa* (1960) and *An African Treasury* (1960) stand as the first significant editions of works by native Africans, and continued for years to be the first point of entry for those in the northern hemisphere. As a result, some regard Hughes as 'the most prolific black-translator of the twentieth century' as well as a 'groundbreaking anthologist'.[18]

After meeting on-duty policeman Sunday Osuya during the party that followed Azikiwe's inauguration, Hughes secured his contact information at an unexpected second encounter the next day. Originally drawn to Osuya's ability to work calmly amid the social chaos, Hughes corresponded frequently with Osuya as time passed. The two met again when the poet returned to Nigeria in December 1961 as well as five years later on another trip. Unexplained by anyone, Hughes even left Osuya a significant sum in his final will.

Because the state is not always the state, Hughes surprisingly became a cultural ambassador to Africa. The naming of journalist Edwin R. Murrow as head of the u.s. Information Agency meant that things the FBI and congressional sub-committees had suspected over the years were of no relevance to a distinctly autonomous body that sought to ease rather than escalate tensions abroad. Murrow, who had successfully undermined McCarthy's power at the height of the 1950s red scare, spoke to Hughes in person about the significance of at least one of his overseas appearances. Always drawn to travel, and appreciative of all things African, Hughes visited Nigeria in 1961 with more than thirty musicians including Lionel Hampton, Randy Weston, Nina Simone and Odetta as part of the American Society for African Culture. On 18 and 19 December he introduced seven of the marquee performers including Hampton, Simone and Odetta.[19] He also appeared in Uganda in 1962, spoke at what Murrow considered a highly significant function in Ghana in 1962 and finally found himself in Senegal for a full month before travelling to Tanzania and Ethiopia in 1966. With a direct reversal to the way Hughes was treated by both the FBI and McCarthy, Hughes's visit with Léopold Sédar Senghor in Senegal was an extension of the relationship that now earned the poet lunch at the White House when the leader, himself a poet, specifically requested Hughes's presence when he visited President Kennedy in November 1961.

After leaving Nigeria in November 1960 Hughes added trips to Italy, France and England before returning to New York. While in London, he was shocked to find that his meeting with the expatriated Richard Wright in Paris had suddenly become the last time anyone would see the writer. Wright died immediately after Hughes's visit, where he showed signs of sickness but nothing suggesting he was critically ill. Hughes brought home many Christmas gifts, most of them from Nigeria. Along with coins, scarves, beads and bracelets for many friends, he also brought ivory birds for both Toy Harper and his first biographer, James Emanuel. Hughes packed a wooden nativity scene he bought in Paris especially for Margaret Bonds.

The wooden nativity is a reminder that Bonds was at the centre of at least two creative endeavours. The pianist and poet started reviving the cantata 'Ballad of the Brown King' before Hughes left. Hughes and Bonds had performed it six years earlier in December 1954 when it was televised by CBS on 'Christmas U.S.A'.[20] Now revised and newly dedicated to Martin Luther King, it was performed by the two on 8 and 11 December in New York to coincide with the Christmas season. More significantly, Bonds accompanied Hughes in February when they successfully debuted *Ask Your Mama: 12 Moods for Jazz* before huge audiences. Hughes had been motivated to write this highly performative work, his first new book of poetry in the last ten years, during his time reflecting on the sad demise of the Newport Jazz Festival. After police had been overrun by a frustrated crowd of mostly white men who could not secure entrance to the sold-out event, Hughes closed out the final session of the festival the next day on 3 July 1960. He would live up to his image of being a spontaneous bluesman by composing 'Goodbye Newport Blues' off-the-cuff and watched as Otis Spann set it to music while Muddy Waters sang. Soon an entire group of musicians joined Hughes on stage to sing what was the festival's swan song.[21]

Hughes delayed returning to New York the next day. Instead, he spent his independence day at the Hotel Viking drafting more than 25 pages of what would become *Ask Your Mamma*. It is difficult to say what the connections between the festival's violent ending and the Fourth of July may have had on the writing. What is certain is the performative nature of poems are more easily heard than read. Hence performances with Bond were met with swelling applause while the printed edition uniformly puzzled and confused readers, both then and today. Hughes had taken on the topic of verbal put-down by invoking the genre of 'playing the dozens' in this work, but not even his extensive musical directives noted throughout the margins could communicate on mere paper how jazz and argument could coalesce. Brilliant as it was, with colours evoking Duke Ellington's album *Black, Brown and Beige* (1958), Hughes's book proved to be mere sheet music that revealed its readers were not musicians.[22] *Ask Your Mama* was meant to be heard, as it was on 16 February 1961 at a world premiere performance with Randy Weston and again two days later at an NAACP event with the Buddy Collette Quintet in Santa Monica.[23] Equally interesting, the Langston Hughes Project, led by University of Southern California music professor Dr Ron McCurdy, created a score based on Hughes's liner notes in 2009 and started performing (and even recorded) a full version of the poem. With trumpet, moving images, bass, piano, drums and spoken word, Hughes's vision has come to life again. 'Mood 6' captures African American life for those who moved to the suburbs as if the section picks up where *A Raisin in the Sun* ends. Moreover, the idea of a child asking his mother for his train fare comes through poignantly in the final 'Mood 12' as Hughes examines every angle of his title.

Partially inspired by his cantata with Margaret Bonds the previous Christmas season, Hughes accepted a commission from Gary Kramer to write *Black Nativity*. Kramer regarded gospel music as a diamond waiting to be polished, and the play highlighted this music so that Hughes's following series of Gospel plays became what some regard as his most 'enduring contribution to American Theatre'.[24] With the play's Broadway debut on 11 December 1961, Hughes unequivocally brought black gospel music to the stage just as his poetry had brought blues to the page. Now, rather than sipping cold drinks at clubs and cafés, Langston was sneaking in and out of local churches throughout Harlem to bring the spirit of black worship to his script. As he told it, he would arrive at around 10 p.m., where 'ancient scripture and contemporary problems were projected with melodic intensity and rhythmic insistence'.[25] Selecting music mostly from the public domain, Hughes allowed minister Alex Bradford to contribute his own melodies and provided ample freedom to the energetic Vinnette Carroll to shape the final script. The play was immediately hailed as 'major entertainment' by both fans and critics.[26] *Black Nativity* represented something special that none of his other dramatic works could, and it was broadcast on ABC TV on Christmas Eve 1962.[27] More importantly, it caught the eye of Gian Carlo Menotti, who, after seeing a production, invited the play to his Festival of Two Worlds held in Spoleto, Italy. Menotti was so persuasive that he secured funding before he had even left the auditorium.[28] Others agreed that the gospel music itself could carry the production well beyond the timeliness of the Christmas season. As such, the play toured throughout Europe, was mounted in Egypt and attended by Hughes in person when he travelled to both London in August 1963 and Berlin in September 1964. It was later made into a motion picture in 2013 starring Forest Whitaker.

After so many scripts, Hughes turned to prose and published his history of the NAACP in 1962. *Fight for Freedom: The Story of the NAACP* reads like a history of lynching in America, reminding readers of the motivation in forming the organization in 1910. As Christopher De Santis has noted, the book contains

> Hughes's unconstrained disgust for the many incidents of racial violence, prejudice and discrimination that motivate the NAACP to act. Hughes gives particular emphasis to the long-term campaign against lynching, often describing in horrific detail the crimes committed to terrorize African Americans into submission.[29]

Mary White Ovington's trips to Alabama in 1906 and then Springfield, Illinois, in 1908, where she learned of lynchings at first hand, drove her to 'remedy the deplorable state of race relations' as she became a founding member of the NAACP.[30]

Hughes wrote with startling detail about such events. In 1919, a man's teeth were sold after his murder for '$5 each and the chain that bound him $0.25 a link'.[31] That the chain itself was used to

bind the victim to a tree while he was burned was just the form
of treatment that had prompted the NAACP's study *Thirty Years of
Lynching in the United States* (1919). Hughes recounts how that study
documents the death of a woman's unborn child after her lynching
as well as the '15,000 men, women, and children' cheering when
they thought Eli Pearson was still alive upon seeing his 'charred
remains move as does meat on a hot frying pan'.[32] Any old tensions
between Hughes's feelings and the organization's stance on class
issues that were conservative as compared with Hughes's own
proletariat views were lost when it came to fighting against such
horrific injustices. In fact, Hughes would soon be commissioned
by the NAACP to write the poem 'Dream of Freedom'. Was Hughes
reminding newcomers such as the Congress on Racial Equality
(CORE), the SNCC and the SCLC that they were wrong to ignore
the NAACP's half century of work fighting against civil rights?
If so, the second stanza can be read as redressing the singularity
communicated by Dr King's dream. Hughes writes against someone
who claims 'This dream for theirs alone –/ A sin for which we know/
They must atone.'[33] Was the reverend's rank as a man of faith being
alluded to when Langston thought of such sin (but not eternal
condemnation) in 1964, or merely dominant culture itself, which
had not yet made space for African Americans?

The book was applauded by members of the organization's legal
defence fund, and Thurgood Marshall himself found that Hughes
had done a marvellous job. Hughes was soon scheduled for more
promotional events than he could attend. They went well. In fact,
Hughes sold nearly five hundred copies when a major event was
held in Cleveland.[34]

When his hour came, Hughes always responded. With the civil
rights movement in full force, he sent off 25 copies of one of his
books to a SNCC official to use in the 'freedom schools' in
Mississippi. He composed a poem for CORE and, at the request
of the NAACP and its desire to celebrate the tenth anniversary of

Brown v. Board of Education, Hughes joined a host of entertainers such as Elizabeth Taylor, Lena Horne, Jackie Gleason and Sammy Davis Jr at Madison Square Garden for a broadcast shown in more than 49 cities.[35] Unfortunately, three colds in the winter of 1962, combined with his age, caused him to swell to an unhealthy size, far wider than his 5'4 frame could carry. At 84 kilograms (185 lb) Hughes was now journeying overseas frequently, where his travelling partner George Bass noted how he often might 'select a place in the midst of each of the ruins or monuments and sit and view the environs without taking another step'.[36] Moreover, Hughes had other reasons to be melancholy, and to some degree he was. He rewrote his will and created clear directives for his funeral service. In some ways he was being immortalized as if he were already dead: French editors selected him (after Whitman, Poe and Dickinson) as the fourth American writer to be featured in the *Poètes d'aujourd'hui* series. A hundred-page critical study of his work by Jean Wagner had appeared in France as well, and his *Selected Poems* was set to appear in Russia.

If others wanted him to be more visible in the movement, that is, march in person rather than only strike with his pen, there was more than Hughes's weight to consider. Hughes was glad to have Malcolm X introduce the revival of his play *Don't You Want to Be Free* in Los Angeles, but *Black Nativity* was 'crippled by an anti-communist smear campaign', and Hughes was still being called an atheist and a communist when a Nashville TV station refused to air an old interview with Hughes. They declared it would be 'an affront to decency'.[37] Banging his fist only once in the presence of George Bass, Hughes's more typical gentleness was both 'deliberate and complex', and Vinnette Carroll recalled that Langston tried to teach her this: 'Always be polite, Vinnette. In fact, be over-polite. Kill them with kindness.'[38] Such kindness seemed to always be on display to emerging writers who sometimes heard: 'Do not be afraid of yourselves. *You* are the world.'[39] When William Melvin

Kelley came to help pack more of Hughes's things for deposit at Yale's Beinecke Library in late February 1962, he left with an autographed copy of *Ask Your Mama* that was in the shape of a record album. Inside, Hughes's published poem 'Cultural Exchange' included opening lines referring to living in homes where there are 'DOORS OF PAPER' to suggest that 'inhabitants are threatened by violence at any time.'[40] Even before the 24-year-old writer, who coined the term 'woke', published his successful debut novel *A Different Drummer* (1962), he read in Hughes's latest book: 'Inscribed especially for William Kelley – on your first visit to my house – welcome!'[41]

11

I Dream a World, 1962–7

As head of the u.s. Information Agency, Edwin R. Murrow personally asked Hughes to speak in Accra, Ghana, on 29 June 1962. The occasion was the dedication of a new American library, to which Hughes donated at least thirty of his own books as well as recordings of his own poetic readings. The purpose was to create a collegial climate between the two nations as America's spokesperson. To successfully accomplish this meant Hughes would have to overlook his own status in his homeland and smile through the irony of being one of its valuable cultural ambassadors. Hughes delivered an address about dreams. His eight-minute talk is reminiscent of ideas that Dr Martin Luther King Jr would invoke on several occasions. In fact, five months before Dr King's first-known 'I Have a Dream' speech would be delivered in Rocky Mount, North Carolina, dreaming was the unifying theme of Hughes's ideas as he asserted this metaphor, but without the flair and unparalleled delivery of the famous preacher.

Hughes began by speaking of the aspirations that unite Africa and America when he said: 'Africa's history, like America's history – and especially the Negro America's history – has been a troubled history, a seeking history, a dreaming history.' He believed that Africa could inspire America as the u.s. was seeking 'a bolstering of its own basic dreams'. He continued by saying that this sharing of knowledge is 'no longer just a dream'. We might imagine how Dr King would perform the lines that Hughes had written.

In a speech that included references to Hughes's poems 'Africa', (1952), 'The Negro Speaks of Rivers' (1921) and 'Words Like Freedom' (1943), the poet ended by customizing his ending to 'Youth' on this special occasion. Often restated by King, and referenced by Azikiwe to end his 1960 ceremony two years earlier, Hughes used the final three (new) lines of the poem to end his address: 'WE MARCH!/ OUR DREAMS TOGETHER,/ WE MARCH!' These thematic parallels ask us to remember that 'King did not simply echo the words Hughes wrote long before the 1960s; he was mirroring the way Hughes was still talking as King's contemporary.'[1]

Hughes continued to make his views on civil rights clear when he sat down for a radio interview with Radio Moscow on 16 May 1963. Events in Birmingham, Alabama, throughout the spring led him to speak out against the vestiges of slavery and the brutality accompanying Jim Crow laws. But he not only spoke against racism in the South, he voiced approval for Dr King's 'humanitarianism', 'decency' and 'love of everyone'.[2] After citing events surrounding Autherine Lucy's entrance to the University of Alabama and James Meredith's enrolment at the University of Mississippi, Hughes went on to call for 'national action that is long overdue', declaring that 'Congress must pass legislation aimed at implementing the Constitution of the United States and the Supreme Court decisions in recent years.'[3] Hughes called for Civil Rights before any bill had even been defined or named.

Though Hughes was willing to speak against racism, other things sometimes interfered with his voice being heard. When writer James Baldwin was asked to organize a meeting for 24 May 1963 between Attorney General Robert Kennedy and several prominent African Americans, Baldwin invited figures such as Lena Horne, Lorraine Hansberry, Harry Belafonte and Rip Torn. Langston Hughes's name was missing from the list of about a dozen figures who would eventually let the meeting deteriorate into shouting and hysteria. Baldwin had no intention of inviting a poet whom he had famously berated in a 29 March 1959 *New York Times* review of *Selected Poems*: 'I am amazed all over again by his genuine gifts – and depressed that he has done so little with them.'[4] Later in life, Baldwin would rescind such an assessment, confessing: 'I hadn't really read the book.'[5] At the time, he may have been responding to Hughes's lukewarm review in 1956 of his own *Notes to a Native Son*. The two would never fully resolve their differences, even bumping into each other on one occasion when Baldwin, 'usually relaxed and philosophical about such occasions', was instead 'strangely embarrassed' as if 'his father had caught him in bad company'.[6] Though the Kennedy meeting would later be hailed as a crucial turning point in the administration's understanding of race relations, Hughes's calm voice was nowhere to be heard.

Langston Hughes learned of the Cuban missile crisis while attending the first-ever National Poetry festival in Washington, DC. Invitations were accepted by 33 poets from Louis Untermeyer, who held a position that would eventually become what is now called U.S. Poet Laureate. After attending a reception hosted by Mrs Kennedy at the White House, where Robert Frost, Louise Bogan, Robert Lowell and others gathered, Hughes sat on a panel the next morning to discuss the topic of 'The Poet and the Public'. In the afternoon session, where he was allotted ten minutes to read, Hughes selected nine poems. He told his audience that a poem 'should be the distilled essence of an emotion – the shorter the better'.[7] After opening with 'Still Here', where he declared that after being 'scared and battered' it was clear 'I'm still here', Hughes continued with poems such as 'The Negro Speaks of Rivers' and 'Merry-Go-Round' before ending with a carefully edited opening section of *Ask Your Mama*.[8] Given the alarming crisis with the Soviet Union, he dropped his references to Moscow in the poem. He also quickly got over his initial anger after he was allotted only one complimentary ticket.

In the end he invited 48 friends, including Frank Reeves as thanks for his past support when speaking before McCarthy almost ten years earlier.[9]

Hughes once again found himself responding to news that concerned justice for African American citizens. He had already published 'Simple's Soliloquy from Hamlet' in the *Chicago Defender*, reminding readers of his alter ego's stance: 'if to be or not to be in jail's/ The question – in jail I'll be.'[10] With events in Birmingham that spring resulting in television and newspaper images of police dogs and fire hoses descending on protesters, a much longer statement – a full draft of Hughes's play *Jericho-Jim Crow* – was finished and bound by 20 June 1963. The play would become 'the most extravagantly praised of Hughes's works in theater'.[11] By the end of the 1960s some theatre critics would note that black drama in America was 'enriched almost single-handedly' by Hughes.[12] Hughes dedicated the play that was his response to the civil rights movement to 'the young people of all racial and religious backgrounds who are meeting, working, canvassing, petitioning, marching, picketing, sitting-in, singing, and praying today to help make a better America for all, and especially for citizens of color'.[13] To capture the shifting tension of oppression through the ages, Hughes wrote the play so that all eight representations of white oppression are played by the same white character. This is a clear act of signifying, as the trickster figure in African American tradition often appears under many guises when cast as a single actor by white playwrights and directors.

Music is once again at the heart of this play by Hughes. Where gospel had anchored *Black Nativity*, new protest songs appear here as singers assert: 'Before I'd be a slave/ I'd be buried in my grave.'[14] More songs follow:

Aint gonna let nobody turn me around
turn me around, turn me around
Aint gonna let nobody turn me around

keep on walkin' keep on talkin'
keep on marchin' to the freedom land.[15]

Like Hughes, Martin Luther King Jr himself clearly understood
the significant relationship between these songs and the Freedom
movement. In a handwritten draft fragment from his book
Why We Can't Wait (1964), King reflected back on the impact
these songs had on the protests in Birmingham in the spring
of 1963:

> It was in the mass meetings also that we sang the Freedom
> Songs. In a sense, the Freedom music is the heart of the
> movement. They are more than just incantations of some
> slick clever phrases designed to invigorate a campaign.
> These Freedom songs are as old as the history of the Negro
> in America . . . I have stood in a meeting with hundreds and
> hundreds of youngsters and joined in the singing: 'Ain't Gonna
> let Nobody Turn me 'Round.' It is not just a song. It is a resolve.
> For minutes later, I have seen those same youngsters refusing
> to turn around before the symbolic threat of a pugnacious
> Bull Connor standing in command of men with power hoses
> of vicious, unreleased pressure.[16]

King is an appropriate voice here as Hughes's complimentary
copies of *Jericho-Jim Crow* made it clear that King was the key source
of inspiration for the play. King's name topped a list of eighteen
recipients who received autographed copies of what Hughes thought
was the finished draft. On 20 June 1963, a mere three days before
King's first nationwide expression of his refrain 'I Have a Dream'
was delivered in Detroit after a 125,000-person march, Hughes
posted an autographed copy of the bound script to King. Written
in his signature green ink, Hughes wrote: 'Especially for Martin
Luther King (whose name – and imprint – is here) with admiration,

Sincerely – Langston Hughes, New York, June 20, 1963.'[17] Four days later, Hughes had made further changes and recalled all eighteen of the earlier drafts of his play, sending new ones in their place to suggest he may have made revisions based on King's speech.[18] What might explain the change?

Jericho-Jim Crow debuted 5 January 1964 at the Sanctuary Theatre in New York City. Near the end of the play, the line 'I dream a land' leads into a re-singing of the play's signature song 'Freedom Land'. The song stood out so much to listeners on opening night that it earned its singer Gilbert Price a laudatory review where he was over-enthusiastically 'hailed as the new Paul Robeson'.[19] The recognized star of a choral group that included Barbra Streisand, the 22-year-old Price soon regarded Hughes as a father figure, and Price received nothing more than heartfelt mentoring from a poet who now 'had a certain reputation' with other men.[20] One reviewer liked the song so well they went so far as to predict that it was 'destined to take its place in the great canon of Negro music'. Though Hughes referred to 'Freedom Land' as 'my song', his words appear to have been set to music by Hughes's assistant George Bass.[21]

In the end, Jericho falls and the walls are tumbling down as W.E.B. Du Bois, Daisy Bates, Jim Peck, A. Philip Randolph, John Lewis, James Farmer, Roy Wilkins, Martin Luther King and John F. Kennedy are those responsible for toppling Jim Crow. In the very last line of the play, we hear 'the promised land's in sight – the America of our dreams!'[22] The pronoun 'our' denotes a collective entrance into the promised land of freedom.

Four days after King's speech in Detroit, on 27 June 1963, Hughes sent a new copy of the revised play to King. Would Hughes dare write anything to let King see that his dream was not his alone? The inscription reads: 'Especially for Martin Luther King, whose name is in this play, Sincerely, Langston Hughes, New York, 1963.' Hughes himself rightly believed that his own poetry had inspired King's dream.[23] Unfortunately, a plan to have a special performance devoted to King himself where the reverend might speak never materialized in 1964.[24]

With the play going strong in April, it moved from New York City to the greater metropolitan area. But the summer months brought reminders of what the play and civil rights movement were fighting for when fifteen-year-old Jimmy Powell was killed by an off-duty white policeman. Rioting and gunfire occurred within earshot of Hughes's home. Hughes attended the viewing for the boy which took place just a few blocks from his own Harlem home. 'Death in Yorkville' captured Hughes's response to injustice that had killed black bodies through slavery, a civil war, lynching and now police shooting. After referencing the recent centennial celebrations surrounding the Emancipation Proclamation, the poem asks: 'How many Centennials does it take/ To kill me,/ Still alive?'[25]

With racial tension and civil rights at the forefront of America's consciousness, Hughes proposed a volume in step with the times. More than happy to remind his publisher that his point of view on race was more relevant than ever, he suggested a volume of poetry featuring his more volatile poems. *Words of Freedom*, he believed, should be offered in a 'cheap, paperback edition to ensure a wide readership'.[26] Knopf declined his offer, believing that the paperback edition would never sell enough copies for them to ever clear a profit. Missing this moment kept Hughes from being more overtly recognized afterwards as an important voice during the height of the civil rights movement. However, three years later, the publisher's representative Judith Jones would consent to everything Hughes had originally suggested. By then 'Birmingham Sunday', Hughes's response to the four girls murdered on 15 September 1963 in Alabama, already seemed outdated. *The Panther and the Lash*, the poet's last book of poetry, took its title from the emergence of the Black Panther Party. When it was published posthumously in 1967, with Hughes having already made all final selections and sequencing of the poems before his death, it included old poems left out of his 1959 *Selected Poems* and also featured new works such as 'Death in Yorkville'. Its titles suggested relevance: 'Black Panther', 'Birmingham Sunday', 'Demonstration', 'Bombings in Dixie', 'War', 'Freedom' and 'Stokely Malcom Me'. However, what once seemed to be too dangerous for Hughes to say, now seemed innocuous when compared with the language invoked by indignant writers such as James Baldwin and LeRoi Jones (Amiri Baraka). Paralleling the boxing world itself, Hughes was the former champion Sonny Liston and these new men were as boisterous as Cassius Clay.

When Hughes started writing a weekly column for the *New York Post* in 1962, the primarily white newspaper looked to Langston Hughes to speak his mind as the leading black writer in the country. This stature can be measured in numerical terms. When the landmark *American Negro Poetry* was released in May 1963, Hughes's entries totalled thirteen poems spread across eleven pages. While most other writers earned no more than four pages, only Robert Hayden and Paul Laurence Dunbar earned more than eight. In 1963 there was Langston Hughes, shadowed by Hayden, and then everyone else when it came to contemporary poetry being written by African Americans. Anchored by Hughes, the volume went through an astonishing eighteen printings and 'disappeared like leaves in a hurricane'.[27] However, Hughes's *Post* columns capture how much difference a year could make. Hughes himself dubbed 1964 'The Jones Year' having seen the plays *Dutchman* and *Baptism*. While Hughes immediately felt the power of the *Dutchman* when he saw it, he soon came to loathe the writer's harsh language and obscene subject-matter. Hughes wrote in his column 'That Boy LeRoi': 'Mr Jones might become America's new Eugene O'Neil – provided he does not knock himself out with pure manure. His current offering, *The Toilet* [is] full of verbal excrement.'[28] Hughes admired Jones's work, but feared what it might mean if the next generation followed his tack. Here Hughes seemed to speak more as a father to those who idolized Jones than as the playwright's own mentor. Nonetheless, works by Hughes and Jones would appear side by side in the *Negro Digest* for the next four years. In short, Hughes was one parent Jones 'need not be ashamed of'.[29]

Hughes was equally critical of James Baldwin in these columns. Baldwin was being reminded that what seemed radical now ignored even recent history. Hughes ended his comments about the writer's latest project *The Fire Next Time* with a reminder of his own chequered past: 'Maybe Baldwin can just cry "Fire", and not have the least idea how to put it out. Or maybe he knows what to do, but will not tell us. Maybe he does not wish to face the next McCarthy.'[30] While the younger writers raised their voices against Hughes, as is expected by established writers from an earlier generation, Hughes was calmly reminding them that he had faced decades of smear campaigns, intimidation and cancelled readings because of his un-American sentiments. The message to the Black Arts Movement was this: the gains made to allow you such freedom of speech had come via the sacrifices made by writers such as Langston Hughes.

When Hughes was not defending Martin Luther King Jr in his *Post* articles, he was explaining the impetus for the violence erupting in his own section of Harlem. On one occasion, he hid for cover, barely avoiding gunfire on Lenox Avenue. Moments later Hughes stood with a gun to his head just outside his home in Harlem while his wallet and watch were stolen. When it came time to write, Hughes sympathized with the plight of his neighbours by comparing them to dogs who have been living on bones but now want meat. With things deteriorating in his neighbourhood, Hughes was more than happy to leave as an emissary of the State Department travelling to Paris, England, Denmark and Germany. One success came when Hughes helped produce an eighteen-part series on 'The Negro in America' for the BBC. Including Hughes's own *Jericho-Jim Crow*, the series was hailed in September 1964 as 'the most important radio event of the year' in England.[31]

It was always hard for Hughes to tell where success would come. He devoted many hours to what seemed the promising enterprise of writing a script about Harlem for Harry Belafonte. The highly influential singer had hit upon the idea after reading Hughes's vivid account of the Harlem Renaissance in *The Big Sea*. Hughes devoted his talents to writing rhymes for Sidney Poitier, knowing he would be strolling through a recreated Harlem of the 1920s. Joined by Sammy Davis Jr and Duke Ellington, 'The Strollin' Twenties' seemed destined to bring praise to all involved as Hughes revised the script throughout 1965. However, an attempt to show another side of a city seemed prepared to fail as violence now erupted across the country. With Watts recently on fire, where more than 34 people had been killed, 1,000 injured and over 3,000 arrested, among property damage of over $40 million in the Los Angeles area, such singing and dancing could not have been planned at a worse time. As such, the television show drew yawns despite lavish sets and star performances when it aired in February 1966. On the other hand, the continued success of *Black Nativity* meant that its Chicago production alone (it was also being staged in London and Berlin) owed Hughes nearly $10,000 in royalties. In the end, as with almost all his theatrical ventures, Hughes had to fight to claim what was his, settling through a lawyer for only $6,900.[32]

Hughes had little trouble understanding the current cost of fighting for civil rights. Malcom X was assassinated in February 1965, and both the murder in Manhattan and the funeral in Harlem were too close to home for Hughes to ignore. Before Hughes's friend Ossie Davis delivered the eulogy to an overflow crowd at Faith Temple of the Church of God in Christ, over 15,000 people filed past the casket in a four-day period of public viewing. What did it mean to teach Hughes in school at this time? Jonathan Kozol was summarily fired from Boston public schools. The Harvard graduate and former Rhodes Scholar made national news when Senator Edward Kennedy spoke out against what had happened in his home state. No one needed to remind Hughes himself of the challenges he faced. When he appeared in Kansas at Wichita State University, the event drew multiple telegrams of protest from four white ministers. Furthermore, school libraries in Oakland, California, held copies of Hughes's tame *Pictorial History of the Negro*, yet lawsuits were threatened if the books were not removed as they were labelled 'communist propaganda'.[33] While intellectuals such as Baldwin and Jones found Hughes too meek and docile for the current age, Hughes was still issuing public statements disavowing he was a communist in vain attempts to claim space on airwaves and bookshelves.

When John Lewis and hundreds of SNCC members attempted to cross the Edmund Pettus Bridge in Montgomery, Alabama, they were met with dogs, clubs and tear gas, and then beaten mercilessly. Dr King soon called for a second and then a third march. King cried after watching President Johnson link the civil rights anthem 'We Shall Overcome' to the direction of America's own goals on a 15 March televised address. Hughes excitedly praised the president directly with a telegram, and the stage seemed set to link SCLC's goals with Hughes's gravitas. As such, King sent Hughes a telegram inviting him to join the final march from Montgomery to Selma.[34]

With Johnson's speech and Hoover's surveillance temporarily decreased, King contacted Hughes without any fear of repercussions. Nonetheless, Hughes refused this invitation for several reasons. His contributions had always been verbal, not physical acts of courage. The trek itself was over 80 kilometres (50 mi.), hardly possible for an overweight 63-year-old man. Combined with the sobering reality of Malcolm X's assassination, Hughes instead channelled his energy through words, writing a column in the *Chicago Defender* that imagined what would happen if Simple went to Selma.[35] But Hughes's presence was felt by the protestors when Coretta Scott King took to the stage. She delivered a dramatic reading of 'Mother to Son' to 10,000 marchers assembled on the final night of the march to hear a host of celebrities perform.[36] When an audience of more than 3,000 in San Francisco heard the performance of Hughes's cantata 'Let Us Remember', it was clear that the events surrounding Selma were not forgotten by Hughes: 'Oh, Remember –/ Montgomery, Selma, and Savannah,/ let not the oppressed become oppressors.'[37]

Readers of the *Chicago Defender* were met by surprising news as 1966 began. Hughes's Simple columns were officially ending. The charmingly delightful alter ego of Hughes was moving with his wife Joyce to the suburbs of Woodlawn. When one thing passed another revived, and when *Street Scene* reopened at the New York City Opera House in February, Hughes attended two performances. If he remembered the frustrations he faced in writing its lyrics, he did not express it outwardly. To all those Hughes came in contact with, he was still regarded for the best traits of his character. With 58 books to his name as author or editor, Alex Haley saw the poet

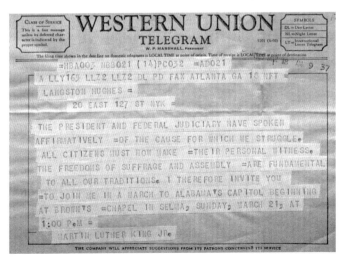

After President Johnson embraced the civil rights movement in a speech delivered 15 March 1965, Dr King invited Hughes by telegram to march from Selma to Montgomery, Alabama, a three-day journey too demanding for Hughes to walk at his age.

Followed the way baseball players are hounded for autographs, Hughes was the brightest star among more than 2,000 guests from fifty different countries at the first World Festival of Negro Arts in Senegal in 1966.

act with 'class'.[38] A prodding Richard Rive could only write in praise after a dinner spent questioning his subject for an article he was writing about Hughes, stating: 'Humility characterizes the truly great.'[39]

A full year removed from linking the presidency with the civil rights movement, Lyndon Johnson could now appoint Langston Hughes as America's official representative to the first World Festival of Negro Arts. Opening 1 April 1966 in Dakar, Senegal, more than 2,000 people gathered from fifty countries to celebrate three weeks of events including performances by Duke Ellington's orchestra. As the leader of over a hundred American representatives, Hughes 'left a mark probably untouched by any single presence other than the president of Senegal himself'. The appointment was one of the top honours of his life, and festival organizer Léopold

Sédar Senghor made Hughes the centre of admiration when he publicly recited 'two obscure poems by Hughes from the '20s'. According to the *New York Times*, Hughes 'emerged as one of the festival's most conspicuous celebrities; young writers from all over Africa followed him about the city and haunted his hotel the way American youngsters dog favorite baseball players'.[40]

Having entertained Wole Soyinka when he visited his Harlem home in 1961, Hughes now spent a memorable final week with Russia's greatest poet, Yevgeny Yevtushenko. Forbidden to read by Senghor because of the festival's focus, Yevtushenko was only lured out of his room when a reporter invited Hughes along to get the Russian to consent to an interview. Their evenings together included heavy drinking, trips in Yevtushenko's limousine and memories where the two men seemed to be arm in arm wherever they went. When it was time for Hughes to take the stage, his topic 'Black Writers in a Troubled World' offered an opportunity for him to use his own poetry to speak out against the obscenity and hatred that were defining the current young writers in America. He shuddered at the thought of black writers 'finger-painting in excrement' for he never dreamed of 'shocking white readers'.[41] Professionalism called Hughes to head the jury for the Grand Prize in the field of English literature, and he overlooked the other extreme of assimilation when he led the selection of Robert Hayden as winner. But even then, Senghor asserted that it was Hughes who was the 'model for the world'.[42]

Brief stops in Ethiopia and Tanzania gave way to an extended one-month stay in Paris. Seeing the likes of Josephine Baker and Henri Cartier-Bresson (to which he had recently dedicated *Simple's Uncle Sam*) renewed in him a sense of wanting to return for even longer stays. After passing up a hit of marijuana at a party, and telling his host later that he 'hated drugs of any kind', Langston was joined by Ted Joans on trumpet when he read his poetry at the Shakespeare and Company bookshop.[43] Across from Notre Dame, and now serving as the gathering place of those who opposed the Vietnam War, the bookshop's crowd was so large Hughes had to defiantly assert his identity just to get in the door.[44] His overseas popularity had swelled in both Africa and France. Being regarded as a relic by some of America's younger writers only encouraged him to travel abroad even more.

More than forty new poems would grace the pages of *The Panther and the Lash* when it appeared posthumously. Knopf had now requested the book it rejected three years earlier, and it sold more than 7,000 copies in the first few months after its release.[45] By some measures, this final collection could be regarded as his most militant since the 1930s.[46] However, when read against what now counted as militancy – the bullhorn cries of 'Black Power' from Stokely Carmichael and the epithets being used against conservative leaders such as Roy Wilkins – the book contained plenty of the right subject-matter, but not the tone of the new era. Hughes addressed the motivation for drug addiction in 'Junior Addict' by reminding readers of the tragedy that 'It's easier to get dope/ than it is to get a job.'[47] 'Death in Yorkville' preceded other sanctioned forms of violence mentioned in poems such as 'Who But the Lord?' where the confused speaker wonders: 'Why God don't protect a man/ from police brutality.'[48] Where the preceding poem ends with a defiant 'we'll see', 'Militant' ends with a fist 'clenched/ today –/ to strike your face'.[49]

In other poems Hughes retells the history of John Brown's raid at Harpers Ferry as well as Jamestown's link to the origins of slavery, and he returns to the lynching poems he left out of *Selected Poems*, with 'Christ in Alabama' and 'Mississippi' both appearing. If 'Cultural Exchange' and its dreams of the 'COLORED HOUR' when 'Martin Luther King is Governor of Georgia' and 'white share-croppers work the black plantations' was not radical enough for readers, it was only because obscenity and murder were excluded.[50] Hughes's selections such as 'Lumumba's Grave' seemed aimed at asking: 'What were those leading the Black Arts Movement doing when Hughes was denouncing the American-sponsored assassination of the Congo's Patrice Lumumba in 1961?' Perhaps in mourning the leader's loss, it was easy to forget that it was Hughes who had seen that American interest in the country's uranium was intimately related to its development of atomic warfare and the reduction of the black world's national leaders to forgotten murder victims. Even the poet's recycled works such as 'Freedom', first published in 1943, contained what could have been rallying cries had they been shouted from makeshift podiums set before rallies, or included on handwritten posters during marches: 'I do not need freedom when I'm dead./ I cannot live on tomorrow's bread.'[51]

The topics Hughes himself had turned into suitable subject matter for poetry were appropriate, but his diction was not volatile enough for contemporary readers. The closest he could come in this vein was in speaking out against the HUAC and the McCarthy Committee where he wrote in 'Un-American Investigations': 'The committee shivers/ With delight in/ Its manure.'[52] Partly because of his age, his now stately position as Dean of African American letters and his fear that the gains of the past were being perverted by writers more motivated by shock value than true anger, Hughes muttered a brief 'You don't/ Give a Damn' in 'Impasse', when stronger four-letter words were being published everywhere.[53]

The pessimistic speaker Hughes chose for his poem 'Promised Land' combined biting wit with hopeless sarcasm. Reactivating the story of Moses' own glimpse into the land he was too afraid to claim, Hughes's eight short lines suggest that such land may indeed be out of reach for now. Hughes ends with the conjunction 'But' as he sees many generations later when the grandchildren of today's children 'will be led/ to a spot from which the Land –/ Still lies ahead.'[54] When Hughes was at his angriest in this era, it was worse than anyone who had seen his smiling face might imagine. 'Bitter Brew' stands as the final poem Hughes ever sent out for publication. Just before his death in 1967, Hughes imagined that his own boiled blood would be reduced to poison. Imagining he was simmered slowly to become an essence of himself, he writes: 'The black poison of me/ To give the white bellies/ The third degree.'[55] No obscenity could be more militant than becoming the very substance that might murder white racists.

Just as he had earlier encouraged and promoted the career of Gwendolyn Brooks through private letters and public reviews, Hughes was proud to have accepted for one of his anthologies, *The Best Short Stories by Negro Writers: An Anthology from 1899 to the Present* (1967), the first story written by Alice Walker. He published 'To Hell with Dying' in the anthology when she was only 21. As such, Hughes felt inclined to confide to Arna Bontemps that 'I can claim her discovery.'[56] Even with Walker's lifelong appreciation for his kindnesses, such happiness did not last long as things at 20 East 127th street were falling apart. The home itself needed major renovations to meet city codes. Owing to the construction and Toy Harper becoming ill, Hughes rented a room at the Hotel Wellington. Langston must have daydreamed about returning to Paris without worries or obligations. In early January, with his home unsettled, he unplugged his phone for an entire weekend.[57] Appearing for Negro History Week at UCLA brought enough sunshine to drive some of his blues away.

Hughes continued to express outward praise for Martin Luther King even while perhaps harbouring some understandable dissatisfaction at having his own contributions overlooked. Actor Fredrick O'Neal wrote to Hughes in 1967: 'I read one or two of your poems at Knoxville College and again last Wednesday at Hampton Institute in a lecture there. I don't know how much Royalty is due, but if this is not sufficient please let me know' 'O'Neal also enclosed a cheque for $10. After thanking O'Neal the same day, a rarity for the poet, who received stacks of correspondence, Hughes raised another subject when he wrote to O'Neal: 'I don't know why Martin Luther King comes to mind (and it never occurred to me to hold it against him) but he has used a poem of mine or two in almost all of his speeches . . . before great big audiences that take up great BIG collections.'[58]

In fact, only eight weeks later, King would indeed again be using Hughes's poetry before another big audience. In the most controversial speech of his life, King named Hughes and then quoted from his 'Let America Be America Again':

Oh, yes,
I say it plain,
America never was America to me,
And yet I swear this oath –
America will be![59]

Hughes and King were linked visually as writer and performer when national television viewers turned on to watch the evening news and saw this clip shown across the country. Hughes stood by King in the aftermath of a speech that forever tarnished King's image because he had dared to speak out against the war, thus jeopardizing the agenda of the civil rights organizers who depended upon federal aid. When King was reduced to tears before his advisors in the aftermath of being denounced from all sides because of this speech, Hughes struck this note to his friend Arna Bontemps: 'At buffet for Loren Miller at the Montero's night before last . . . Roy Wilkins, Best Granger, etc. all so *mad* with Martin Luther's they could Klux him. Me no! I Love him.'[60] Hughes leaves out the words 'King' and 'speech' after 'Luther's', and others' anger is poetically highlighted in the use of 'Klux' as a substitute for 'kill'.

Hughes had planned to be in Paris in May 1967. Working on a written request from Harry Belafonte, Hughes felt a severe pain that did not lessen. Fifteen hours later he was admitted to New York Polyclinic and assigned to a urologist. Ignoring painful urination that had plagued him for the previous two months, Hughes checked in, to avoid any recognition, with the name of his father, 'James Hughes'. The two interns who examined him feared prostate cancer when a mass was discovered near his bladder. The bladder was badly infected, but not cancerous, so surgery for the still unrecognized and uninsured patient was scheduled for 12 May. Hughes prepared for his first-ever operation and the death he feared by assigning his assistant Raoul Abdul to complete several final tasks. Frustrated, Hughes ended an unusually rare and heated exchange with his assistant by requesting the poetry volume *One-way Ticket*, though his assistant was unaware of any reason why this was the specific one he requested at such a personal moment.[61] With orders to alert no one other than Arna Bontemps, and to turn away anyone who dared to attempt a visit, another more profound artefact still remains a mystery.

From his deathbed, Hughes sent Martin Luther King Jr a handwritten letter that has never been found. Did King destroy it based on its contents? Did Hughes explain why he had kept his distance from King and SCLC? Did Hughes in any way suggest he deserved at least some credit for King's own dream, or was Hughes merely encouraging the leader, as he had so often, as King's prestige had fallen catastrophically after he publicly denounced the Vietnam War? Was the letter merely lost during an especially hectic era at SCLC headquarters? As of now, we have only the postcard reply dated 17 May that acknowledges receipt of Hughes's letter: 'Your letter came during Dr King's absence from the city. He is scheduled to return to the Atlanta office in about ten days, at which time your correspondence will be brought to his attention for reply.'[62] What did Hughes say? Why is the letter missing from all of King's files?

Surviving both the surgery and a vasectomy, Hughes also had pneumonia that required medical treatment, and penicillin was

From his deathbed, one of the very last things Hughes did was send a handwritten letter to Dr King. King's secretary Dora McDonald here acknowledges receipt of this letter that has yet to be found (May 1967).

Mr. Langston Hughes
20 East 127th Street

New York 35, New York

Southern Christian Leadership Conference
334 Auburn Avenue, N. E.
Atlanta, Georgia 30303

Dear Mr. Hughes:

Your letter came during Dr. King's absence from the city. He is scheduled to return to the Atlanta office in about ten days, at which time your correspondence will be brought to his attention for reply.

(Miss) D. McDonald
Secretary to Dr. Martin Luther King, Jr.

prescribed three days later. Five days after the operation, Hughes was critically ill. Moved to the hospital's Intensive Care Unit and placed on dialysis, Langston Hughes fell into a brief coma before dying of what was deemed 'septic shock' late in the evening of 22 May. The stunning news was featured the next day on the front page of the *New York Times*.

Hughes's funeral service was an unforgettable event to those who attended. Forgetful of his wishes of an entirely closed casket, Hughes was placed on view both the day before and on the morning of the service. But true to his detailed plans, Randy Weston and two other musicians played a selection of old and original blues songs, ending with Duke Ellington's 'Do Nothin' Till You Hear From Me'. As the final section of the programme, people genuinely did not know whether to laugh, remain seated or get up and leave. Hughes deliberately chose this song to capture some of Harlem's odd and unsettling traditions. During the 1920s, outrageous funerals such as those for A'Lelia Walker and Florence Mills became outlandish events featuring men standing on caskets or with aeroplanes releasing blackbirds overhead.[63] In fact, even the refined Alain Locke propped up his deceased mother on a parlour couch in 1922 so that she looked like a hostess receiving guests to her own wake.[64] For those too nervous to laugh at his final musical jest, Hughes's signature poem 'I Dream a World' remained printed in the programme for them to read.

Hughes's body was cremated, and his remains reside in a public place beneath a marvellous cosmogram located in the floor of the Schaumburg Center in his beloved Harlem. Based on Hughes's greatest place references, the circling symbols feature lines from 'The Negro Speaks of Rivers'. Honouring the spirit of his era, Amiri Baraka bent to an imposing Maya Angelou, each dancing the jitterbug over Hughes, when he was formally interned at the centre in 1991. Within the circle of people surrounding them, everyone was laughing, but not to keep from crying, and they all knew whose shoulders they were standing on.

Epilogue

To preview the historic opening of the National Museum of African American History and Culture in 2016, the *New York Times* devoted an entire page to reprinting Hughes's poem 'I, Too'.[1] The *New York Times* and other media outlets highlighted Hughes's words after receiving private tours in advance of the museum's opening where they felt the impact of 'I, Too, Am America', these four words appearing inside the museum with unmistakable prominence behind a blue and gold aeroplane used by Tuskegee airmen during the Second World War. With the entire poem below, Hughes's words hang in giant brass letters above the history galleries and have the final wall all to themselves.

Hughes could hardly have imagined that the city where he was 'discovered' as a 'Bus Boy' poet would one day showcase such an unmistakable visual marker celebrating African American excellence. The poem was also reprinted in the *New York Times* because it best foreshadowed what was to come two days later on 24 September 2016, at the museum's grand opening ceremonies on the National Mall in Washington, DC. When the reverend Dr Calvin O. Butts III took the microphone to welcome guests that included three presidents (and a national television audience), the words listeners heard were from 'My People': 'The night is beautiful,/ So the faces of my people.'[2] This was followed by his clumsy recitation of 'Notes on Commercial Theater', where he misspoke and referenced 'movies', something not mentioned anywhere in the poem. Trying to recall the correct lines from memory, the experienced speaker invoked some pseudo-suave humour as he named Oprah Winfrey, his eye catching her seated in the immediate audience. When he suddenly remembered part of the ending to Hughes's poem, he stumbled free from an overlooked error. Butts would soon allude to Hughes's 'Let America Be America Again' by riffing off the campaign slogan of then Republican candidate Donald J. Trump by saying 'Make America Great, O Yes' before imploring the audience to 'Hold on to your dreams' just as Hughes himself had done in his poem 'Dreams'.[3]

When museum director Lonnie Bunch stepped up to the podium on the most important day of his career, it soon became clear that Will Smith's earlier recitation of 'Dream Deferred' and Reverend Butts's lines were but an extension of his own passions. A sigh that was both relief and joy ended when the carefully chosen first words came from Bunch's lips: 'Today a dream too long deferred is a dream no longer.'[4]

All that was left was for President Obama himself to riff on a few lines of Hughes, or name a poem or two, and the occasion would have Langston's bow tie wrapped around the building's remarkable design. What no one could have expected is that, instead of simply nodding to Hughes, President Obama chose him for his muse in what is perhaps the only substantive speech by a sitting u.s. president to be unified by a single poem.

After only a few short paragraphs, the president was telling listeners that 'All of us are American.'[5] To be sure everyone understood his allusion, the president solemnly spoke: 'I, too, am America,' then took a three-second pause to let the words reverberate.[6] Closing his remarks that day with the final line 'We, too, are America,' the president turned Hughes's archetypal 'I' into a collective 'We', allowing what the singular had always represented to become more accessible.[7] In different genres, these two African American titans were saying exactly the same thing. As such, Hughes's relevance seems certain: he will continue to be appropriated and beloved as people continue to make news with his poetry.

References

Prologue

1 Milton Meltzer, *Langston Hughes: A Biography* (New York, 1968), p. 252.
2 Langston Hughes, *The Collected Poems of Langston Hughes*, ed. Arnold Rampersad and David Roessel (New York, 1994), p. 32.
3 Ibid., p. 311.
4 Ibid., p. 426.
5 Langston Hughes, *Selected Letters of Langston Hughes*, ed. Arnold Rampersad and David Roessel (New York, 2015), p. 321.

1 Motherless Child, 1901–19

1 Jennifer Schuessler, 'Langston Hughes Just Got a Year Older', *New York Times* (9 August 2018), p. c1.
2 Faith Berry, *Langston Hughes: Before and Beyond the Harlem Renaissance* (New York, 1996), p. 1.
3 Arnold Rampersad, *The Life of Langston Hughes* (New York, 2002), vol. i, p. 4.
4 Ibid., p. 13.
5 Ibid., pp. 6–7.
6 Ibid., p. 12.
7 Langston Hughes, *Remember Me to Harlem: The Letters of Langston Hughes and Carl Van Vechten, 1925–1964*, ed. Emily Bernard (New York, 2001), p. 12.
8 Langston Hughes, *The Big Sea* (New York, 1993), p. 209.
9 Rampersad, *Life*, vol. i, pp. 12–13.

10 Milton Meltzer, *Langston Hughes: A Biography* (New York, 1968), p. 12.

11 Rampersad, *Life*, vol. I, p. 5.

12 Berry, *Hughes: Before and Beyond*, p. 9.

13 Langston Hughes, *The Collected Poems of Langston Hughes*, ed. Arnold Rampersad and David Roessel (New York, 1994), p. 23.

14 Berry, *Hughes: Before and Beyond*, p. 11.

15 Rampersad, *Life*, vol. I, p. 17.

16 Hughes, *Collected Poems*, p. 86.

17 Hughes, *The Big Sea*, pp. 20–21.

18 Wallace D. Best, *Langston's Salvation: American Religion and the Bard of Harlem* (New York, 2017), p. 56.

19 Ibid., p. 169.

20 Ibid., p. 15.

21 Hughes, *The Big Sea*, p. 24.

22 Rampersad, *Life*, vol. I, p. 24.

23 Hughes, *Collected Poems*, p. 198.

24 Hughes, *The Big Sea*, p. 34.

25 Rampersad, *Life*, vol. I, p. 30.

26 Berry, *Hughes: Before and Beyond*, pp. 14–15.

27 Meltzer, *A Biography*, p. 36.

28 James Emanuel, *Langston Hughes* (Boston, MA, 1967), p. 21.

29 Hughes, *The Big Sea*, p. 33.

30 Best, *Salvation*, p. 16.

31 Langston Hughes Papers, Sartur Andrzewski, letter to Langston Hughes (30 March 1923), Box 8, Folder 166, Beinecke Library, James Weldon Johnson Collection, Yale University, New Haven, CT.

32 Hughes, *Collected Poems*, p. 30.

2 I, Too, Am America, 1919–24

1 Langston Hughes, *The Big Sea* (New York, 1993), p. 47.

2 Langston Hughes Papers, 'A Diary of Mexican Adventures' (20 July 1920), Box 492, Folder 12432, Beinecke Library, James Weldon Johnson Collection, Yale University, New Haven, CT.

3 Langston Hughes, *The Collected Poems of Langston Hughes*, ed. Arnold Rampersad and David Roessel (New York, 1994), p. 23.

4 Milton Meltzer, *Langston Hughes: A Biography* (New York, 1968), p. 255.
5 W. Jason Miller, *Langston Hughes and American Lynching Culture* (Gainesville, FL, 2011), pp. 34–5.
6 Ibid., p. 38.
7 Leslie Pinckney Hill, 'My Race', *Crisis*, XXIII/1 (1921), p. 29.
8 Laurie Leach, *Langston Hughes: A Biography* (Westport, CT, 2004), p. 133.
9 Langston Hughes Papers, Langston Hughes, letter to W.E.B. Du Bois (22 May 1956), Box 57, Folder 1073, Beinecke Library, James Weldon Johnson Collection, Yale University, New Haven, CT.
10 James Emanuel, *Langston Hughes* (Boston, MA, 1967), p. 151.
11 Arnold Rampersad, *The Life of Langston Hughes* (New York, 2002), vol. II, pp. 178, 425.
12 Rampersad, *Life*, vol. I, p. 49.
13 Ibid., p. 42.
14 Ibid., p. 51.
15 Langston Hughes, *Remember Me to Harlem: The Letters of Langston Hughes and Carl Van Vechten, 1925–1964*, ed. Emily Bernard (New York, 2001), p. 32.
16 Faith Berry, *Langston Hughes: Before and Beyond the Harlem Renaissance* (New York, 1996), p. 28.
17 Rampersad, *Life*, vol. I, p. 52.
18 Berry, *Hughes: Before and Beyond*, p. 29.
19 Ibid., p. 31.
20 Hughes, *Collected Poems*, p. 597.
21 Ibid., p. 32.
22 Berry, *Hughes: Before and Beyond*, p. 33.
23 Hughes, *Collected Poems*, p. 30.
24 W. Jason Miller, 'Foregrounding and Prereading: Using Langston Hughes's Poetry to Teach *A Raisin in the Sun*', *Notes on American Literature,* XXIV/1 (Spring 2012), p. 5.
25 Hughes, *Collected Poems*, p. 50.
26 Rampersad, *Life*, vol. I, p. 66.
27 Leach, *Langston Hughes*, p. 79.
28 Rampersad, *Life*, vol. I, p. 78.
29 Ibid., p. 79.

30 Langston Hughes Papers, Langston Hughes, notes (1930), Box 492, Folder 12432, Beinecke Library, James Weldon Johnson Collection, Yale University, New Haven, CT.

31 Hughes, *Collected Poems*, p. 36.

32 Rampersad, *Life*, vol. I, p. 81.

33 Hughes, *The Big Sea*, p. 160.

34 Ibid., p. 178.

35 T. Denean Sharpley-Whiting, *Bricktop's Paris* (Albany, NY, 2015), p. 30.

36 Ibid., pp. 30–31.

37 Rampersad, *Life*, vol. I, p. 90.

38 Hughes, *Collected Poems*, p. 305.

39 Berry, *Hughes: Before and Beyond*, p. 53.

40 Ibid., p. 117.

41 Hughes, *Collected Poems*, p. 46.

42 Leach, *Langston Hughes*, p. 67.

43 Rampersad, *Life*, vol. I, p. 98.

44 Ibid.

3 A Bone of Contention, 1924–30

1 Arnold Rampersad, *The Life of Langston Hughes* (New York, 2002), vol. I, p. 101.

2 Langston Hughes, *The Big Sea* (New York, 1993), p. 206.

3 Rampersad, *Life*, vol. I, p. 107.

4 Faith Berry, *Langston Hughes: Before and Beyond the Harlem Renaissance* (New York, 1996), p. 62.

5 Rampersad, *Life*, vol. I, p. 109.

6 Ibid., p. 110.

7 Ibid., p. 116.

8 Ibid., p. 117.

9 Ibid., pp. 123–4.

10 James Emanuel, *Langston Hughes* (Boston, MA, 1967), p. 146.

11 Langston Hughes, *Remember Me to Harlem: The Letters of Langston Hughes and Carl Van Vechten, 1925–1964*, ed. Emily Bernard (New York, 2001), p. 159.

12 Langston Hughes, *The Collected Poems of Langston Hughes* (New York, 1994), p. 72.

13 Barbara Foley, 'Questionnaire Responses', *Modernism/Modernity*, XX/3 (2013), p. 440.

14 Berry, *Hughes: Before and Beyond*, p. 79.

15 Ibid., p. 78.

16 Wallace Thurman, *Infants of the Spring* (Boston, MA, 1932), p. 232.

17 Berry, *Hughes: Before and Beyond*, p. 76.

18 George Schyler, 'The Negro-art Hokum', *The Nation*, CXXIII (1926), p. 662.

19 Langston Hughes, 'The Negro Artist and the Racial Mountain', *The Nation*, CXXIII (1926), p. 692.

20 Amy Helen Kirschke, *Aaron Douglas: Art, Race, and the Harlem Renaissance* (Jackson, MS, 1995), pp. 78–9.

21 W.E.B. DuBois, 'What Is Civilization? – Africa's Answer', *Forum* LXXIII/2 (1925), p. 8.

22 Hughes, 'The Negro Artist', p. 694.

23 Ibid.

24 Ibid.

25 Rampersad, *Life*, vol. I, p. 145.

26 Ibid., p. 144.

27 John P. Shields, 'Never Cross the Divide: Reconstructing Langston Hughes's *Not Without Laughter*', *African American Review*, XXVIII/4 (1994), p. 603.

28 Milton Meltzer, *Langston Hughes: A Biography* (New York, 1968), p. 140.

29 Barbara Burkhardt, 'The Blues in Langston Hughes's *Not Without Laughter*', *Midamerica: The Yearbook of the Society for the Subject of Midwestern Literature*, XXIII/1 (1996), p. 116.

30 Steven C. Tracy, *Langston Hughes and the Blues* (Urbana, IL, 1988), p. 27.

31 Langston Hughes, *The Collected Works of Langston Hughes*, ed. Arnold Rampersad et al. (Columbia, MO, 2001–4), vol. IV, p. 129.

32 Ibid., p. 148.

33 Joan Stone, 'Circles of Liberation and Constriction: Dance in *Not Without Laughter*', in *Montage of a Dream Deferred: The Art and Life of Langston Hughes,* ed. John Edgar Tidwell and Cheryl R. Ragar (Columbia, MO, 2007), p. 275.

34 Shields, 'Never Cross the Divide', p. 609.

35 Berry, *Hughes: Before and Beyond*, p. 94.
36 Langston Hughes Papers, Langston Hughes, unpublished speech 'Humor and the Negro Press', 10 January 1957, Box 481, Folder 12123, Beinecke Library, James Weldon Johnson Collection, Yale University, New Haven, CT.
37 Langston Hughes, *Selected Letters of Langston Hughes*, ed. Arnold Rampersad and David Roessel (New York, 2015), pp. 89–90.
38 Rampersad, *Life*, vol. I, p. 171.
39 Ibid., p. 179.
40 Ibid., p. 178.
41 Frank Andre Guridy, *Forging Diaspora* (Chapel Hill, NC, 2010), p. 139.
42 Vera M. Kutzinski, *The Worlds of Langston Hughes: Modernism and Translation in the Americas* (Ithaca, NY, 2012), p. 58.
43 Ibid., p. 57.
44 Hughes, *Selected Letters*, p. 109.
45 Langston Hughes Papers, Langston Hughes, unpublished poem 'Batabano' (1930), Box 492, Folder 124326, Beinecke Library, James Weldon Johnson Collection, Yale University, New Haven, CT.
46 Langston Hughes Papers, Langston Hughes, unpublished poem 'Momento Habanero' (1930), Box 492, Folder 124326, Beinecke Library, James Weldon Johnson Collection, Yale University, New Haven, CT.
47 Langston Hughes Papers, Langston Hughes, unpublished poem 'A Million Miles' (6 August 1941), Box 381, Folder 6680, Beinecke Library, James Weldon Johnson Collection, Yale University, New Haven, CT.
48 Eve Sedgwick, *Epistemology of the Closet* (Berkeley, CA, 1990), p. 45.
49 Shane Vogel, *The Scene of Harlem Cabaret* (Chicago, IL, 2009), p. 104.
50 Berry, *Hughes: Before and Beyond*, p. 347, note 10.
51 Andrew Donnelly, 'Langston Hughes on the DL', *College Literature*, XXXXIV/1 (2017), p. 37.
52 Wallace D. Best, *Langston's Salvation: American Religion and the Bard of Harlem* (New York, 2017), p. 15.
53 Vogel, *Harlem Cabaret*, p. 36.
54 T. Denean Sharpley-Whiting, *Bricktop's Paris* (Albany, NY, 2015), p. 46.
55 Vogel, *Harlem Cabaret*, p. 187.
56 Donnelly, 'Hughes on the DL', p. 39.
57 Yuval Taylor, *Zora and Langston: A Story of Friendship and Betrayal* (New York, 2019), p. 171.

58 Langston Hughes, *Letters from Langston: From the Harlem Renaissance to the Red Scare and Beyond*, ed. Louise Evelyn Crawford and Marylouise Patterson (Oakland, CA, 2016), p. 33.

59 Hughes, *The Big Sea*, p. 325.

60 Taylor, *Zora and Langston*, p. 138.

61 Rampersad, *Life*, vol. I, p. 185.

62 Berry, *Hughes: Before and Beyond*, p. 343, note 3.

63 Rampersad, *Life*, vol. I, p. 195.

64 Ibid., p. 196.

65 Taylor, *Zora and Langston*, p. 176.

66 Berry, *Hughes: Before and Beyond*, p. 116.

67 Rampersad, *Life*, vol. I, p. 198.

68 Hughes, *The Big Sea*, p. 333.

69 Ibid., p. 327.

70 Arna Bontemps, *Arna Bontemps–Langston Hughes Letters, 1925–1967*, ed. Charles H. Nichols (New York, 1980), p. 44.

71 Rampersad, *Life*, vol. I, p. 199.

4 In the USSR, 1930–33

1 Langston Hughes Papers, Langston Hughes, unpublished poem 'Capitalism' (n. d.), Box 375, Folder 6664, Beinecke Library, James Weldon Johnson Collection, Yale University, New Haven, CT.

2 W. Jason Miller, *Origins of the Dream: Hughes's Poetry and King's Rhetoric* (Gainesville, FL, 2015), p. 33.

3 Langston Hughes, *The Collected Poems of Langston Hughes*, ed. Arnold Rampersad and David Roessel (New York, 1994), p. 174.

4 Nancy Cunard, 'Scottsboro and Other Scottsboros', in *Witnessing Lynching: American Writers Respond*, ed. Anne Rice (New Brunswick, NJ, 2007), p. 273.

5 Hughes, *Collected Poems*, p. 142.

6 Wilson Library, Langston Hughes, letter to Milton Abernathy (22 October 1931), Guy Johnson Collection, Contempo Records, Series 1, Folder 47, University of North Carolina, Chapel Hill, NC.

7 W. Jason Miller, *Langston Hughes and American Lynching Culture* (Gainesville, FL, 2011), p. 52.

8 Ibid., pp. 60–63, 55.

9 Ibid., pp. 53–4.

10 Langston Hughes, *Selected Letters of Langston Hughes*, ed. Arnold Rampersad and David Roessel (New York, 2015), p. 120.

11 W. Jason Miller, 'Hughes and Lynching', in *Critical Insights: Langston Hughes*, ed. R. Baxter Miller (Ipswich, MA, 2013), p. 163.

12 Hughes, *Collected Poems*, p. 168.

13 Wilson Library, Langston Hughes, poem 'The Town of Scottsboro' (22 October 1931), Guy Johnson Collection, Contempo Records, Series 1, Folder 47, University of North Carolina, Chapel Hill, NC.

14 Langston Hughes, *Remember Me to Harlem: The Letters of Langston Hughes and Carl Van Vechten, 1925–1964*, ed. Emily Bernard (New York, 2001), p. 93.

15 Milton Meltzer, *Langston Hughes: A Biography* (New York, 1968), p. 151.

16 Arnold Rampersad, *The Life of Langston Hughes* (New York, 2002), vol. I, p. 215.

17 Ibid., p. 232.

18 Bonnie Greer, *Langston Hughes: The Value of Contradictions* (London, 2011), p. 142.

19 Eric J. Sundquist, *Cultural Contexts for Ralph Ellison's 'Invisible Man'* (Boston, MA, 1995), p. 65.

20 Miller, *American Lynching Culture*, p. 42.

21 Rampersad, *Life*, vol. I, p. 233.

22 Ibid., p. 229.

23 Langston Hughes, *The Collected Works of Langston Hughes*, ed. Dianne Johnson (Columbia, MO, 2001–4), vol. XI, p. 145.

24 Ibid., p. 147.

25 Ibid.

26 Hughes, *Collected Poems*, p. 32.

27 Langston Hughes, 'Those Who Have No Turkey', in *The Brownies' Book* (1921), p. 194.

28 Langston Hughes, *Letters from Langston: From the Harlem Renaissance to the Red Scare and Beyond*, ed. Louise Evelyn Crawford and Marylouise Patterson (Oakland, CA, 2016), p. 63.

29 Rampersad, *Life*, vol. I, p. 219.

30 Hughes, *Remember Me to Harlem*, p. 105.

31 Langston Hughes, 'Advertisement for the Waldorf Astoria', in *Anthology of American Poetry* (Oxford, UK, 2001), p. 1231.

32 Rampersad, *Life*, vol. I, p. 241.

33 Faith Berry, *Langston Hughes: Before and Beyond the Harlem Renaissance* (New York, 1996), p. 157.

34 Ibid., p. 156.

35 Ibid., p. 159.

36 Ibid., p. 168.

37 Ibid., p. 170.

38 Rampersad, *Life*, vol. I, pp. 262, 268.

39 Letitia Guran, 'Insurgent Hughes: Negotiating Multiple Narratives Digitally', *MELUS*, XXXXII/4 (2017), p. 30.

40 Robert Robinson, *Black on Red: My 44 Years inside the Soviet Union* (Washington, DC, 1988), p. 321.

41 Hughes, *Collected Poems*, p. 163.

42 Ibid., p. 176.

43 Berry, *Before and Beyond*, p. 176.

44 Guran, 'Insurgent Hughes', p. 136.

45 Hughes, *Letters from Langston*, p. 110.

46 Rampersad, *Life*, vol. I, p. 268.

47 Ibid., pp. 271–2.

48 Ibid., p. 209.

49 Ibid., p. 265.

50 Ibid., p. 264.

51 Berry, *Before and Beyond*, p. 187.

52 Hughes, *Selected Letters*, p. 157.

53 Ibid., p. 164.

54 Rampersad, *Life*, vol. I, p. 288.

55 Berry, *Before and Beyond*, p. 277.

56 Ibid., p. 182.

57 Hughes, *Letters from Langston*, p. 115.

58 Berry, *Before and Beyond*, p. 180.

59 Ibid., p. 195.

60 Ibid., pp. 197–8.

5 Let America Be America Again, 1933–40

1 Arnold Rampersad, *The Life of Langston Hughes* (New York, 2002), vol. I, pp. 276–7.
2 Ibid., pp. 269–70.
3 Ibid., p. 238.
4 Ibid., pp. 281–2.
5 Langston Hughes, *Langston Hughes: Short Stories*, ed. Donna Akiba Sullivan Harper (New York, 1996), p. vii.
6 James Emanuel, *Langston Hughes* (Boston, MA, 1967), p. 102.
7 W. Jason Miller, *Langston Hughes and American Lynching Culture* (Gainesville, FL, 2011), p. 135.
8 Faith Berry, *Langston Hughes: Before and Beyond the Harlem Renaissance* (New York, 1996), p. 202.
9 Hughes, *Short Stories*, p. xvii.
10 Berry, *Before and Beyond*, p. 216.
11 Rampersad, *Life*, vol. I, p. 294.
12 Langston Hughes, *The Collected Works of Langston Hughes*, ed. Joseph McLaren (Columbia, MO, 2001–4), vol. XIV, p. 283.
13 Berry, *Before and Beyond*, p. 225.
14 Ibid., pp. 235–6.
15 Langston Hughes, *Remember Me to Harlem: The Letters of Langston Hughes and Carl Van Vechten, 1925–1964*, ed. Emily Bernard (New York, 2001), p. 129.
16 Berry, *Before and Beyond*, p. 230.
17 Ibid., p. 232.
18 Rampersad, *Life*, vol. I, pp. 312–13.
19 Langston Hughes, *I Wonder as I Wander* (New York, 1956), p. 310.
20 Rampersad, *Life*, vol. I, p. 312.
21 Ibid., p. 319.
22 Ibid., p. 315.
23 Emanuel, *Hughes*, p. 109.
24 Milton Meltzer, *Langston Hughes: A Biography* (New York, 1968), p. 84.
25 Hughes, *The Collected Poems of Langston Hughes*, ed. Arnold Rampersad and David Roessel (New York, 1994), p. 58.
26 Meltzer, *A Biography*, p. 197.

27   R. Baxter Miller, *The Art and Imagination of Langston Hughes* (Lexington, KY, 1989), p. 119.

28   Miller, *American Lynching Culture*, p. 134.

29   Ibid.

30   Langston Hughes, *Collected Poems*, p. 189.

31   Ibid.

32   Rampersad, *Life*, vol. I, p. 320.

33   Langston Hughes, *Letters from Langston: From the Harlem Renaissance to the Red Scare and Beyond*, ed. Louise Evelyn Crawford and Marylouise Patterson (Oakland, CA, 2016), p. 214.

34   Hughes, *Collected Poems*, p. 311.

35   W. Jason Miller, *Origins of the Dream: Hughes's Poetry and King's Rhetoric* (Gainesville, FL, 2015), p. 145.

36   Emanuel, *Hughes*, p. 129.

37   Langston Hughes, 'Mister Sandman', in *The Brownies' Book* (1921), p. 244.

38   Langston Hughes, *Good Morning Revolution: Uncollected Writings of Social Protest*, ed. Faith Berry (Secaucus, NJ, 1992), p. 98.

39   Ibid., p. 130.

40   Rampersad, *Life*, vol. I, p. 332.

41   Ibid., pp. 332–3.

42   Ibid., p. 332.

43   Ibid., p. 333.

44   Berry, *Before and Beyond*, p. 279.

45   Rampersad, *Life*, vol. I, p. 334.

46   Berry, *Before and Beyond*, pp. 262–3.

47   Meltzer, *A Biography*, p. 209.

48   Emanuel, *Hughes*, p. 37.

49   Berry, *Before and Beyond*, pp. 262–3.

50   Ibid., p. 257.

51   Meltzer, *A Biography*, p. 214.

52   Hughes, *Collected Poems*, p. 202.

53   Hughes, *Letters from Langston*, p. 134.

54   Berry, *Before and Beyond*, p. 254.

55   Hughes, *Collected Poems*, p. 207.

56   Ibid., p. 306.

57   Berry, *Before and Beyond*, p. 266.

58   Ibid.

59 Ibid.

60 Hughes, *I Wonder*, p. 362.

61 Ibid., p. 363.

62 Berry, *Before and Beyond*, p. 267.

63 Ibid., p. 269.

64 Rampersad, *Life*, vol. I, pp. 357–8.

65 Meltzer, *A Biography*, p. 221.

66 Rampersad, *Life*, vol. I, p. 360.

67 Hughes, *Letters from Langston*, p. 161.

68 Berry, *Before and Beyond*, p. 275.

69 Rampersad, *Life*, vol. I, p. 359.

70 Ibid., p. 356.

71 Langston Hughes Papers, Langston Hughes, poem 'August 19th' (1937–8), Box 373, Folder 6125, Beinecke Library, James Weldon Johnson Collection, Yale University, New Haven, CT.

72 Langston Hughes, 'August 19', *The Daily Worker* (28 June 1938), p. 7.

73 Langston Hughes Papers, 'August 19th'.

74 Ibid.

75 Berry, *Before and Beyond*, p. 345, note 10.

76 Rudolph Castown, *The Daily Worker* (28 June 1938), p. 6.

77 Clarence Norris and Sybil D. Washington, *Last of the Scottsboro Boys: An Autobiography* (New York, 1979), p. 173.

78 Langston Hughes Papers, 'August 19th'.

79 Ibid.

80 Carrie Hughes, *My Dear Boy: Carrie Hughes's Letters to Langston Hughes*, ed. Carmaletta M. Williams and John Edgar Tidwell (Athens, GA, 2013), p. 112.

81 Ibid.

82 Ibid., pp. 166–8.

83 Ibid., p. 51.

84 Langston Hughes, *The Big Sea* (New York, 1993), p. 12.

85 Steven Lubet and Rachel Maines, 'This Shawl Belonged to Langston Hughes (True) and Was Worn by One of John Brown's Men at Harpers Ferry (Well . . .)', *Humanities*, XXXVII/3 (2016), p. 5.

86 Ibid., p. 8.

87 Ibid., p. 10.

88 Ibid., p. 9.

89 Ibid., p. 3.
90 Ibid., p. 11.
91 Hughes, *Collected Poems*, p. 142.
92 Thomas Cripps, 'Langston Hughes and the Movies: The Case of *Way Down South*', in *Montage of a Dream: The Art and Life of Langston Hughes*, ed. John E. Tidwell and Cheryl R. Ragar (Columbia, MO, 2007), p. 309.
93 David Chinitz, *Which Sin to Bear? Authenticity and Compromise in Langston Hughes* (New York, 2013), p. 231, note 3.
94 Hughes, *Letters from Langston*, p. 165.
95 Rampersad, *Life*, vol. I, p. 371.
96 Hughes, *Letters from Langston*, p. 152.
97 Chinitz, *Which Sin to Bear?* p. 87.

6 Aimee B. Simple, 1940–45

1 Milton Meltzer, *Langston Hughes: A Biography* (New York, 1968), p. 224.
2 Ibid., p. 228.
3 Arnold Rampersad, *The Life of Langston Hughes* (New York, 2002), vol. I, p. 373.
4 Ibid., p. 374.
5 Langston Hughes, *Remember Me to Harlem: The Letters of Langston Hughes and Carl Van Vechten, 1925–1964*, ed. Emily Bernard (New York, 2001), p. 176.
6 Langston Hughes, *The Big Sea* (New York, 1993), p. 56.
7 Rampersad, *Life*, vol. I, p. 377.
8 Ibid., p. 379.
9 Hughes, *The Big Sea*, p. xxv.
10 Ibid., p. XVII.
11 Ibid., p. 109.
12 Rampersad, *Life*, vol. I, p. 389.
13 Ibid., p. 388.
14 Ibid., p. 382.
15 Ibid., p. 386.
16 William J. Maxwell, *F. B. Eyes* (Princeton, NJ, 2015), p. 237.
17 Langston Hughes, *The Collected Poems of Langston Hughes*, ed. Arnold Rampersad and David Roessel (New York, 1994), p. 212.

18 Rampersad, *Life*, vol. I, p. 390.

19 Meltzer, *Langston Hughes*, p. 236.

20 Hughes, *Collected Poems*, p. 166.

21 Rampersad, *Life*, vol. I, p. 390.

22 Faith Berry, *Langston Hughes: Before and Beyond the Harlem Renaissance* (New York, 1996), p. 295.

23 Rampersad, *Life*, vol. I, p. 390.

24 Wallace D. Best, *Langston's Salvation: American Religion and the Bard of Harlem* (New York, 2017), p. 120.

25 Rampersad, *Life*, vol. I, p. 393.

26 Langston Hughes, *Letters from Langston: From the Harlem Renaissance to the Red Scare and Beyond*, ed. Louise Evelyn Crawford and Marylouise Patterson (Oakland, CA, 2016), pp. 202–3.

27 Best, *Langston's Salvation*, p. 122.

28 Ibid., p. 123.

29 Langston Hughes, *Good Morning Revolution: Uncollected Writings of Social Protest*, ed. Faith Berry (Secaucus, NJ, 1992), p. 134.

30 Berry, *Before and Beyond*, p. 296.

31 Hughes, *Letters from Langston*, p. 202.

32 Hughes, *Remember Me to Harlem*, p. 168.

33 Meltzer, *Langston Hughes*, p. 231.

34 Hughes, *Letters from Langston*, p. 242.

35 Hughes, *Collected Poems*, p. 215.

36 Ibid., p. 240.

37 W. Jason Miller, *Origins of the Dream: Hughes's Poetry and King's Rhetoric* (Gainesville, FL, 2015), p. 71.

38 Langston Hughes, *Selected Letters of Langston Hughes*, ed. Arnold Rampersad and David Roessel (New York, 2015), p. 245.

39 Hughes, *Collected Poems*, p. 269.

40 Ibid., p. 289.

41 Arnold Rampersad, *The Life of Langston Hughes* (New York, 2002), vol. II, pp. 57–8.

42 Ibid., p. 71.

43 Hughes, *Collected Poems*, p. 264.

44 Christopher De Santis, *Langston Hughes and the Chicago Defender* (Champaign, IL, 1995), p. 13.

45 Ibid., p. 41.

46 Ibid., p. 98.

47 Ibid., p. 149.

48 Ibid., p. 60.

49 Donna Akiba Sullivan Harper, *Not So Simple: The 'Simple' Stories by Langston Hughes* (Columbia, MO, 1995), p. 78.

50 De Santis, *Hughes and the Defender*, p. 15.

51 James Emanuel, *Langston Hughes* (Boston, MT, 1967), p. 155.

52 Laurie Leach, *Langston Hughes: A Biography* (Westport, CT, 2004), p. 122.

53 Emanuel, *Langston Hughes*, p. 177.

54 Ibid., p. 44.

55 Ibid., p. 177.

56 Rampersad, *Life*, vol. II, p. 71.

57 Miller, *American Lynching Culture*, p. 79.

58 Hughes, *Selected Letters*, p. 241.

7 F. B. Eyes, 1945–50

1 Fred Kaplan, 'Cécile McLroin Salvant's Timeless Jazz', *New Yorker* (22 May 2017), p. 34.

2 Arnold Rampersad, *The Life of Langston Hughes* (New York, 2002), vol. II, pp. 107–9.

3 Ibid., pp. 109–10.

4 Langston Hughes, *Remember Me to Harlem: The Letters of Langston Hughes and Carl Van Vechten, 1925–1964*, ed. Emily Bernard (New York, 2001), p. 186.

5 Langston Hughes, *Selected Letters of Langston Hughes*, ed. Arnold Rampersad and David Roessel (New York, 2015), p. 306.

6 Rampersad, *Life*, vol. II, pp. 124–5.

7 Hughes, *Remember Me to Harlem*, p. 221.

8 Rampersad, *Life*, vol. II, pp. 126–7.

9 William J. Maxwell, *F. B. Eyes* (Princeton, NJ, 2015), p. 18.

10 Ibid., p. 20.

11 Ibid., pp. 234–6.

12 Langston Hughes, *The Collected Poems of Langston Hughes*, ed. Arnold Rampersad and David Roessel (New York, 1994), pp. 13–14.

13 W. Jason Miller, *Origins of the Dream: Hughes's Poetry and King's Rhetoric* (Gainesville, FL, 2015), p. 41.

14 Ibid.

15 J. Edgar Hoover, 'Secularism – A Breeder of Crime' (1947), Manuscript Archives, Special Collections, J. Willard Marriott Library, University of Utah, Salt Lake City, p. 6.

16 Maxwell, *F. B. Eyes*, pp. 168–9.

17 Hughes, *Collected Poems*, p. 338.

18 Ibid., p. 358.

19 *Billboard* (30 August 1947), p. 31.

20 Langston Hughes Papers, Langston Hughes, *The Freedom Train and Other Poems* (18 February 1953), Box 330, Folder 4934, Beinecke Library, James Weldon Johnson Collection, Yale University, New Haven, CT.

21 Hughes, *Collected Poems*, p. 338.

22 Langston Hughes Papers, *The Freedom Train and Other Poems*.

23 Hughes, *Collected Poems*, p. 324.

24 Judith Anne Still, *Just Tell the Story – Troubled Island* (Flagstaff, AZ, 2006), p. 277.

25 Ibid., p. 521.

26 Langston Hughes, *Letters from Langston: From the Harlem Renaissance to the Red Scare and Beyond*, ed. Louise Evelyn Crawford and Marylouise Patterson (Oakland, CA, 2016), p. 281.

27 Still, *Just Tell the Story*, p. 282.

28 Ibid., p. 93.

29 Ibid., p. 129.

30 Ibid., p. 522.

31 William Grant Still, *Troubled Island*, World Premiere Performance, New York City Opera, 31 March 1949 (Flagstaff, AZ, 1999).

32 Rampersad, *Life*, vol. II, p. 166.

33 Still, *Just Tell the Story*, p. 316.

34 Rampersad, *Life*, vol. II, p. 166.

35 Ibid.

36 Still, *Just Tell the Story*, p. 87.

37 Ibid., p. 105.

38 Rampersad, *Life*, vol. II, p. 167.

39 Still, *Just Tell the Story*, p. 105.

40 Ibid., p. 107.

41 'Dupes and Fellow Travelers Dress Up Communist Fronts', *Life* (4 April 1949), pp. 41–2.
42 Rampersad, *Life*, vol. II, p. 168.

8 Montage of a Dream Deferred, 1950–53

1 Arnold Rampersad, *The Life of Langston Hughes* (New York, 2002), vol. II, p. 185.
2 Ibid., p. 182.
3 Rampersad, *Life*, vol. II, p. 185.
4 Langston Hughes, *The Collected Poems of Langston Hughes*, ed. Arnold Rampersad and David Roessel (New York, 1994), p. 407.
5 Shane Vogel, *The Scene of Harlem Cabaret* (Chicago, IL, 2009), p. 116.
6 Hughes, *Collected Poems*, p. 406.
7 Megan Marshall, *Elizabeth Bishop* (New York, 2017), p. 86.
8 Hughes, *Collected Poems*, p. 406.
9 Julien Roebuck and Wolfgang Reese, *The Rendezvous: A Case Study of an Afterhours Club* (New York, 1976), p. 257.
10 Steven C. Tracy, 'Without Respect for Gender: Damnable Inference in "Blessed Assurance"', in *Critical Insights: Langston Hughes*, ed. R. Baxter Miller (Ipswich, MA, 2013), p. 223.
11 Hughes, *Collected Poems*, 'Island', p. 429.
12 For successful discussions of Hughes's use of 'montage', see *Montage of a Dream: The Art and Life of Langston Hughes*, ed. John Edgar Tidwell and Cheryl R. Ragar (Columbia, MO, 2007), and Bartholomew Brinkman, 'Movies, Modernity, and All That Jazz: Langston Hughes's *Montage of a Dream Deferred*', *African American Review*, XXXIV/1–2 (Spring/Summer 2011), pp. 85–96.
13 Jonathan Scott, *Socialist Joy in the Writing of Langston Hughes* (Columbia, MO, 2006), p. 165.
14 Sara Blair, *Harlem Crossroads: Black Writers and the Photograph in the Twentieth Century* (Princeton, NJ, 2007), p. 54.
15 W. Jason Miller, *Langston Hughes and American Lynching Culture* (Gainesville, FL, 2011), p. 100.
16 Rampersad, *Life*, vol. II, pp. 244, 249.

17 Peter Galassi, *Roy DeCarava: A Retrospective* (New York, 1996), p. 20.

18 Langston Hughes Papers, Langston Hughes, letters to Roy DeCarava (7 March 1955 and 1 March 1956), Box 53, Folder 994, Beinecke Library, James Weldon Johnson Collection, Yale University, New Haven, CT.

19 Rampersad, *Life*, vol. II, p. 338.

20 Faith Berry, *Langston Hughes: Before and Beyond the Harlem Renaissance* (New York, 1996), pp. 230-1.

21 Langston Hughes, *Selected Letters of Langston Hughes*, ed. Arnold Rampersad and David Roessel (New York, 2015), p. 323.

22 Rampersad, *Life*, vol. II, p. 128.

23 Blair, *Harlem Crossroads*, p. 54.

24 Janet Zandy, *Unfinished Stories: The Narrative Photography of Hansel Mieth and Marion Palfi* (Rochester, NY, 2013), p. 87.

25 Langston Hughes Papers, Marion Palfi, letter to Langston Hughes (25 June 1952), Box 126, Folder 2360, Beinecke Library, James Weldon Johnson Collection, Yale University, New Haven, CT.

26 Langston Hughes Papers, Marion Palfi, letter to Langston Hughes (31 May 1964), Box 126, Folder 2358, Beinecke Library, James Weldon Johnson Collection, Yale University, New Haven, CT.

27 Langston Hughes Papers, Marion Palfi, letter to Langston Hughes (31 March 1963), Box 126, Folder 2362, Beinecke Library, James Weldon Johnson Collection, Yale University, New Haven, CT.

28 Zandy, *Unfinished Stories*, p. 119.

29 Blair, *Harlem Crossroads*, p. 54.

30 Zandy, *Unfinished Stories*, p. 135.

31 Miller, *American Lynching Culture*, p. 100.

32 Hughes, *Collected Works*, vol. VII, p. 228.

33 Ibid.

34 Hughes, *Collected Poems*, p. 420.

35 Ibid., p. 409.

36 Rampersad, *Life*, vol. II, p. 153.

37 Cary Nelson, *Anthology of American Poetry* (Oxford, 2000), p. 502.

38 Langston Hughes Papers, Langston Hughes, drafts of 'Dream Deferred' (1948), Box 316, Folder 5155, Beinecke Library, James Weldon Johnson Collection, Yale University, New Haven, CT.

39 Ibid.

40 Ibid.

41 W. Jason Miller, *Origins of the Dream: Hughes's Poetry and King's Rhetoric* (Gainesville, FL, 2015), p. 86.

42 Langston Hughes Papers, Langston Hughes, letter to Lorraine Hansberry (5 April 1958), Box 74, Folder 1426, Beinecke Library, James Weldon Johnson Collection, Yale University, New Haven, CT.

43 Langston Hughes Papers, Claudia McNeil, letter to Langston Hughes (20 March 1959), Box 110, Folder 2052, Beinecke Library, James Weldon Johnson Collection, Yale University, New Haven, CT.

44 Langston Hughes Papers, Langston Hughes, letter to 'Melba' (16 February 1961), Box 177, Folder 3252, Beinecke Library, James Weldon Johnson Collection, Yale University, New Haven, CT.

45 Langston Hughes Papers, Langston Hughes, notes for radio appearance (April 1960), Box 482, Folder 12156, Beinecke Library, James Weldon Johnson Collection, Yale University, New Haven, CT.

46 W. Jason Miller, 'Langston Hughes's Hidden Influence on MLK', www.theconversation.com (30 March 2018).

47 Barack Obama, 2008 Acceptance Speech, www.nytimes.com (28 August 2008).

48 W. Jason Miller, '"Don't Turn Back": Langston Hughes, Barack Obama, and Martin Luther King, Jr.', *African American Review*, XXXXVI/2–3 (Autumn 2013), p. 435.

49 Miller, *Origins of the Dream*, p. 18.

9 Seeing Red, 1953–60

1 Langston Hughes Papers, Joseph R. McCarthy, letter to Langston Hughes (21 March 1953), Box 365, Folder 5862, Beinecke Library, James Weldon Johnson Collection, Yale University, New Haven, CT.

2 Arnold Rampersad, *The Life of Langston Hughes* (New York, 2002), vol. II, p. 208.

3 Ibid., p. 195.

4 Vera M. Kutzinski, *The Worlds of Langston Hughes: Modernism and Translation in the Americas* (Ithaca, NY, 2012), p. 191.

5 David Chinitz, *Which Sin to Bear? Authenticity and Compromise in Langston Hughes* (New York, 2013), p. 115.

6 Ibid., p. 113.

7   Ibid., p. 136.

8   Ibid., p. 121.

9   Ibid., p. 198.

10 Ibid., p. 126.

11 Faith Berry, *Langston Hughes: Before and Beyond the Harlem Renaissance* (New York, 1996), p. 318.

12 Chinitz, *Which Sin to Bear?*, p. 128.

13 Ibid., p. 131.

14 Langston Hughes Papers, Langston Hughes, statement to the Senate (23 March 1953), Box 365, Folder 5862, Beinecke Library, James Weldon Johnson Collection, Yale University, New Haven, CT.

15 Langston Hughes Papers, Langston Hughes, 'I Dream a World' (n.d.), Box 365, Folder 5887, Beinecke Library, James Weldon Johnson Collection, Yale University, New Haven, CT.

16 W. Jason Miller, *Origins of the Dream: Hughes's Poetry and King's Rhetoric* (Gainesville, FL, 2015), p. 147.

17 Rampersad, *Life*, vol. II, p. 218.

18 Miller, *Origins of the Dream*, p. 41.

19 Rampersad, *Life*, vol. II, p. 218.

20 Berry, *Hughes: Before and Beyond*, p. 319.

21 Chinitz, *Which Sin to Bear?*, p. 110.

22 Langston Hughes Papers, Langston Hughes, letter to Frank Reeves (8 April 1953), Box 136, Folder 2525, Beinecke Library, James Weldon Johnson Collection, Yale University, New Haven, CT.

23 Berry, *Hughes: Before and Beyond*, p. 319.

24 Rampersad, *Life*, vol. II, p. 221.

25 Cary Nelson, *Revolutionary Memory: Recovering the Poetry of the American Left* (New York, 2003), p. 68.

26 Langston Hughes, *Remember Me to Harlem: The Letters of Langston Hughes and Carl Van Vechten, 1925–1964*, ed. Emily Bernard (New York, 2001), p. 277.

27 Christopher Metress, 'Langston Hughes's "Mississippi-1955": A Note on Revisions and an Appeal for Reconsideration', *African American Review*, XXXVII/1 (2003), p. 147.

28 Miller, *Origins of the Dream*, p. 80.

29 Langston Hughes, 'Let's Organize as Well as Mobilize, Says Simple', *Chicago Defender* (8 June 1957), p. 10.

30 Miller, *Origins of the Dream*, pp. 81–2.

31 Langston Hughes, *The Collected Works of Langston Hughes*, ed. Leslie Catherine Sanders, vol. VI (Columbia, MO, 2001–4), p. 472.

32 Langston Hughes, *Letters from Langston: From the Harlem Renaissance to the Red Scare and Beyond*, ed. Louise Evelyn Crawford and Marylouise Patterson (Oakland, CT, 2016), p. 304.

33 Miller, *Origins of the Dream*, p. 30.

34 Rampersad, *Life*, vol. II, p. 281.

35 Langston Hughes, 'Simple Says Acting Right Is Better Than Writing Right', *Chicago Defender* (23 June 1957), p. 10.

36 Langston Hughes Papers, Langston Hughes, 'Humor and the Negro Press' (10 January 1957), Box 481, Folder 12123, Beinecke Library, James Weldon Johnson Collection, Yale University, New Haven, CT.

37 Ibid.

38 Langston Hughes, 'Simple as President of All People', *Chicago Defender* (25 May 1963), p. 8.

39 Rampersad, *Life*, vol. II, p. 258.

40 Ibid., pp. 259–60.

41 Ibid., p. 262.

42 Langston Hughes, *Arna Bontemps–Langston Hughes Letters, 1925–1967*, ed. Charles H. Nichols (New York, 1980), p. 378.

43 W. Jason Miller, *Langston Hughes and American Lynching Culture* (Gainesville, FL, 2011), p. 124.

44 Langston Hughes, *The Collected Poems of Langston Hughes*, ed. Arnold Rampersad and David Roessel (New York, 1994), p. 440.

45 Ibid., p. 24.

46 Langston Hughes Papers, Langston Hughes, 'The Negro' (January 1959), Box 381, Folder 6714, Beinecke Library, James Weldon Johnson Collection, Yale University, New Haven, CT.

47 Ibid.

48 Ibid.

49 W. Jason Miller, 'Hughes and Lynching', in *Critical Insights: Langston Hughes*, ed. R. Baxter Miller (Ipswich, MA, 2013), p. 172.

50 Hughes, *Arna Bontemps–Langston Hughes Letters*, p. 408.

51 Ibid.

52 Elizabeth Alexander, *The Black Interior* (St Paul, MN, 2004), p. 21.

10 Bright Tomorrows, 1960–62

1 W. Jason Miller, *Origins of the Dream: Hughes's Poetry and King's Rhetoric* (Gainesville, FL, 2015), p. 100.

2 W. Jason Miller, 'Foregrounding and Prereading: Using Langston Hughes's Poetry to Teach *A Raisin in the Sun*', *Notes on American Literature*, XXIV/1 (2012), p. 10.

3 Langston Hughes Papers, Martin Luther King Jr, letter to Langston Hughes (30 November 1959), Box 96, Folder 1806, Beinecke Library, James Weldon Johnson Collection, Yale University, New Haven, CT.

4 Langston Hughes Papers, Langston Hughes, calendars (1960), Box 491, Beinecke Library, James Weldon Johnson Collection, Yale University, New Haven, CT.

5 Langston Hughes Papers, Langston Hughes, telegram to Ruby Dee (25 January 1960), Box 53, Folder 997, Beineice Library, James Weldon Johnson Collection, Yale University, New Haven, CT.

6 Langston Hughes, *The Collected Works of Langston Hughes*, ed. Arnold Rampersad et al. (Columbia, MO, 2001–4), vol. III, p. 118.

7 Langston Hughes Papers, Langston Hughes, phone logs (10 June 1960), Box 502, Folder 12572, Beinecke Library, James Weldon Johnson Collection, Yale University, New Haven, CT.

8 Taylor Branch, *Parting the Waters: America in the King Years, 1954–63* (New York, 1989), p. 345.

9 Langston Hughes, *Letters from Langston: From the Harlem Renaissance to the Red Scare and Beyond*, ed. Louise Evelyn Crawford and Marylouise Patterson (Oakland, CA, 2016), p. 182.

10 W. Jason Miller, 'Langston Hughes and Martin Luther King: Together in Nigeria', *South Atlantic Review*, LXXXIII/1 (2018), p. 34.

11 Miller, *Origins of the Dream*, p. 149.

12 Ibid., p. 75.

13 Ibid., p. 97.

14 Ibid., p. 214.

15 Ibid., p. 4.

16 Ibid., p. 123.

17 Miller, 'Hughes and King: Together in Nigeria', p. 29.

18 Brent Edwards, *The Practice of Diaspora: Literature, Translation, and the Rise of Black Internationalism* (Cambridge, MA, 2003), p. 59.

19 Arnold Rampersad, *The Life of Langston Hughes* (New York, 2002), vol. II, p. 348.

20 Faith Berry, *Langston Hughes: Before and Beyond the Harlem Renaissance* (New York, 1996), p. 315.

21 Rampersad, *Life*, vol. II, p. 315.

22 James Emanuel, *Langston Hughes* (Boston, MA, 1967), p. 165.

23 Langston Hughes Papers, Langston Hughes, *Ask Your Mama* (16 February 1961), Box 483, Folder 12231, Beinecke Library, James Weldon Johnson Collection, Yale University, New Haven, CT.

24 Hughes, *Collected Works*, vol. VI, p. 353.

25 Ibid.

26 Rampersad, *Life*, vol. II, p. 347.

27 Hughes, *Collected Works*, vol. VI, p. 354.

28 Rampersad, *Life*, vol. II, p. 349.

29 Hughes, *Collected Works*, vol. X, p. 15.

30 Ibid., p. 39.

31 Ibid., p. 51.

32 Ibid., p. 53.

33 Langston Hughes, *The Collected Poems of Langston Hughes*, ed. Arnold Rampersad and David Roessel (New York, 1994), p. 542.

34 Rampersad, *Life*, vol. II, p. 357.

35 Ibid., p. 377.

36 Ibid., p. 366.

37 Ibid., p. 368.

38 Ibid., p. 368.

39 Milton Meltzer, *Langston Hughes: A Biography* (New York, 1968), p. 257.

40 Jean Wagner, *Black Poets of the United States: From Paul Lawrence Dunbar to Langston Hughes* (Urbana, IL, 1973), p. 461.

41 Kathryn Schulz, 'The Lost Giant of American Literature', *New Yorker* (29 January 2018), p. 26.

11 I Dream a World, 1962–7

1 W. Jason Miller, *Origins of the Dream: Hughes's Poetry and King's Rhetoric* (Gainesville, FL, 2015), p. 213.

2 Langston Hughes Papers, Langston Hughes, Radio Moscow (16 May 1963), Box 483, Folder 12231, Beinecke Library, James Weldon Johnson Collection, Yale University, New Haven, CT.

3 Ibid.

4 Arnold Rampersad, *The Life of Langston Hughes*, vol. II (New York, 2002), p. 295.

5 Ibid., p. 299.

6 Ibid., p. 298.

7 James Emanuel, *Langston Hughes* (Boston, MA, 1967), p. 127.

8 Rampersad, *Life*, vol. II, p. 367.

9 Langston Hughes Papers, Langston Hughes, National Poetry Festival (24 October 1962), Box 483, Folder 12225, Beinecke Library, James Weldon Johnson Collection, Yale University, New Haven, CT.

10 Langston Hughes, *Letters from Langston: From the Harlem Renaissance to the Red Scare and Beyond*, ed. Louise Evelyn Crawford and Marylouise Patterson (Oakland, CA, 2016), p. 327.

11 Langston Hughes, *The Collected Works of Langston Hughes*, ed. Leslie Catherine Sanders (Columbia, MO, 2001–4), vol. VI, p. 254.

12 Emanuel, *Langston Hughes*, p. 40.

13 Hughes, *Collected Works*, vol. VI, p. 254.

14 Ibid., p. 264.

15 Ibid., p. 258.

16 Howard Gotlieb Archival Research Center, Dr. Martin Luther King Jr. Collection, Box 22, Folder 1, Boston University, Boston, MA.

17 Miller, *Origins of the Dream*, p. 208.

18 Ibid.

19 Hughes, *Collected Works*, vol. VI, p. 254.

20 Rampersad, *Life*, vol. II, pp. 372–3.

21 Ibid., p. 372.

22 Hughes, *Collected Works*, vol. VI, p. 279.

23 Nibir K. Ghosh, 'A Soul Deep Like the Rivers: Re-visiting Langston Hughes with Arnold Rampersad', *Re-Markings*, XIII/1 (2014), p. 39.

24 Langston Hughes Papers, Langston Hughes, *Jericho-Jim Crow* (1964), Box 379, Folder 5060, Beinecke Library, James Weldon Johnson Collection, Yale University, New Haven, CT.

25 Langston Hughes, *The Collected Poems of Langston Hughes*, ed. Arnold Rampersad and David Roessel (New York, 1994) p. 554.

26 Rampersad, *Life*, vol. II, p. 376.

27 Langston Hughes, *Arna Bontemps–Langston Hughes Letters, 1925–1967*, ed. Charles H. Nichols (New York, 1980), p. 487.

28 Rampersad, *Life*, vol. II, p. 383.

29 Onwuchekwa Jemie, *Langston Hughes: An Introduction to the Poetry* (New York, 1976), p. 186.

30 Ibid., p. 375.

31 Faith Berry, *Langston Hughes: Before and Beyond the Harlem Renaissance* (New York, 1996), pp. 256–7.

32 Rampersad, *Life*, vol. II, p. 379.

33 Ibid., p. 387.

34 Langston Hughes Papers, Martin Luther King Jr, telegram to Langston Hughes (18 March 65), Box 96, Folder 1806, Beinecke Library, James Weldon Johnson Collection, Yale University, New Haven, CT.

35 Langston Hughes, 'If Simple Went to Selma', *Chicago Defender* (24 April 1965), p. 8.

36 Miller, *Origins of the Dream*, p. 29.

37 Rampersad, *Life*, vol. II, p. 395.

38 Ibid., p. 399.

39 Ibid.

40 Ibid., p. 400.

41 Ibid., p. 402.

42 Ibid., p. 403.

43 Ibid., p. 407.

44 Ibid., p. 408.

45 Milton Meltzer, *Langston Hughes: A Biography* (New York, 1968), p. 252.

46 Berry, *Hughes: Before and Beyond*, p. 327.

47 Hughes, *Collected Poems*, p. 539.

48 Ibid., p. 322.

49 Ibid., p. 131.

50 Ibid., p. 480.

51 Ibid., p. 289.

52 Ibid., p. 560.

53 Ibid., p. 458.

54 Ibid., p. 592.

55 Ibid., p. 617.

56 Langston Hughes, *Selected Letters of Langston Hughes*, ed. Arnold
    Rampersad and David Roessel (New York, 2015), p. 415.

57 Rampersad, *Life*, vol. II, p. 415.

58 Langston Hughes Papers, Langston Hughes, letter to Fredrick O'Neal
    (8 February 1967), Box 123, Folder 2319, Beinecke Library, James
    Weldon Johnson Collection, Yale University, New Haven, CT.

59 Hughes, *Collected Poems*, p. 191.

60 Langston Hughes, *Arna Bontemps–Langston Hughes Letters*, p. 486.

61 Rampersad, *Life*, vol. II, p. 422.

62 Langston Hughes Papers, Dora McDonald, postcard to Langston
    Hughes (17 May 1967), Box 96, Folder 1806, Beinecke Library, James
    Weldon Johnson Collection, Yale University, New Haven, CT.

63 Emanuel, *Langston Hughes*, p. 29.

64 Tobi Haslett, 'Black Orpheus', *New Yorker* (12 May 2018), p. 91.

Epilogue

1 Langston Hughes, 'I, Too', *New York Times* (22 September 2016), p. F8.

2 Langston Hughes, *The Collected Poems of Langston Hughes*, ed. Arnold
   Rampersad and David Roessel (New York, 1994), p. 36.

3 Grand Opening Dedication Ceremony, www.nmaahc.si.edu
   (24 September 2016).

4 Ibid.

5 Ibid.

6 Ibid.

7 Ibid.

Further Reading

Works by Hughes

Poetry

The Weary Blues (1926)
Fine Clothes to the Jew (1927)
Shakespeare in Harlem (1942)
Fields of Wonder (1947)
One-way Ticket (1949)
Montage of a Dream Deferred (1951)
Selected Poems of Langston Hughes (1959)
Ask Your Mama: 12 Moods for Jazz (1961)
The Panther and the Lash: Poems for Our Times (1967)
The Collected Poems of Langston Hughes (1994)

Fiction

Not Without Laughter (1930)
The Ways of White Folks (1934)
Simple Speaks His Mind (1950)
Laughing to Keep from Crying (1952)
Simple Takes a Wife (1953)
The Sweet Flypaper of Life (1955)
Simple Stakes a Claim (1957)
The Best of Simple (1961)
Something in Common and Other Stories (1963)
Simple's Uncle Sam (1965)

Autobiography

The Big Sea (1940)
I Wonder as I Wander (1956)

Collected Works

Hughes, Langston, *The Collected Works of Langston Hughes*, ed. Arnold
Rampersad et al., 16 vols (Columbia, MO, 2001–4)

Letters

Bernard, Emily, ed., *Remember Me to Harlem: The Letters of Langston Hughes
and Carl Van Vechten, 1925–1964* (New York, 2001)
Crawford, Louise Evelyn, and Marylouise Patterson, eds, *Letters from
Langston: From the Harlem Renaissance to the Red Scare and Beyond*
(Berkley, CA, 2016)
Nichols, Charles H., ed., *Arna Bontemps–Langston Hughes Letters, 1925–1967*
(New York, 1980)
Rampersad, Arnold, and David Roessel, eds, *The Selected Letters of Langston
Hughes* (New York, 2015)
Williams, Carmaletta M., and John Edgar Tidwell, eds, *My Dear Boy: Carrie
Hughes's Letters to Langston Hughes, 1926–1938* (Athens, GA, 2013)

Works about Hughes

Berry, Faith, *Langston Hughes: Before and Beyond the Harlem Renaissance*
(New York, 1983)
—, ed., *Good Morning Revolution: Uncollected Writings of Social Protest*
(New York, 1973)
Best, Wallace D., *Langston's Salvation: American Religion and the Bard of
Harlem* (New York, 2017)
Chinitz, David, *Which Sin to Bear? Authenticity and Compromise in Langston
Hughes* (New York, 2013)
De Santis, Christopher C., ed., *Langston Hughes and the Chicago Defender,
1942–62* (Urbana, IL, 1995)
Emanuel, James, *Langston Hughes* (Boston, MA, 1967)

Harper, Donna Akiba Sullivan, *Not So Simple: The 'Simple' Stories by Langston Hughes* (Columbia, MO, 1995)

Kutzinski, Vera M., *The Worlds of Langston Hughes: Modernism and Translation in the Americas* (Ithaca, NY, 2012)

Meltzer, Milton, *Langston Hughes: A Biography* (New York, 1968)

Miller, R. Baxter, *The Art and Imagination of Langston Hughes* (Lexington, KY, 1989)

—, ed., *Critical Insights: Langston Hughes* (Athens, GA, 2012)

Miller, W. Jason, *Langston Hughes and American Lynching Culture* (Gainesville, FL, 2011)

—, *Origins of the Dream: Hughes's Poetry and King's Rhetoric* (Gainesville, FL, 2015)

Rampersad, Arnold, *The Life of Langston Hughes*, 2 vols (New York, 1986, 1988)

Taylor, Yuval, *Zora and Langston: A Story of Friendship and Betrayal* (New York, 2019)

Tidwell, John Edgar, and Cheryl R. Ragar, eds, *Montage of a Dream Deferred: The Art and Life of Langston Hughes* (Columbia, MO, 2007)

Tracy, Steven C., *Langston Hughes and the Blues* (Urbana, IL, 1988)

Journal

Bolden, Tony, ed., *The Langston Hughes Review* (University Park, PA, 1981–)

Acknowledgements

Scholarship brings us into contact with people who alter our perspectives on the subject at hand. I have benefited from primary sources supplied by Dolores Colon, Anne Marie Menta and Natalia Sciarini at Yale University's Beinecke Rare Book and Manuscript Library. Bob Anthony's leadership as curator and director of the University of North Carolina at Chapel Hill's North Carolina Collection and Digital Heritage Center has allowed me to benefit from artefacts located and prepared by Tim Hodgdon and Jessica Kincaid. Under the remarkable leadership of Greg Raschke and expert programming of Marian Fragola, library staff at NC State University such as Michael Fairback, Justin Haynes and Alex Valencia imaged hard-to-find documents. Equally important support on its campus was made possible by Sachelle Ford, Moses T. Alexander Greene, Angela Jenkins and Toni Thorpe at the African American Cultural Center.

Permission to use parts of Hughes's work were secured by Maggie Auffarth at Harold Ober Associates and Chris Aguirre at Penguin Random House. Among this ever-growing field of study, I wish to thank Hughes scholars Faith Berry, Wallace Best, David Chinitz, Christopher C. De Santis, James Emanuel, Donna Akiba Sullivan Harper, Onwuchekwa Jemie, Vera Kutzinski, Milton Meltzer, R. Baxter Miller, Arnold Rampersad, John Edgar Tidwell, Steven Tracy, Jean Wagner, and Carmaletta Williams. My work would not be possible without all these exceptional scholars. Distinguished officers of the Langston Hughes Society, Tara Green, Richard Hancuff, Dolan Hubbard, Sharon Lynette Jones and Christopher Allen Varlack have generously connected me with many exciting scholars such as Tracy Sharpley-Whiting. I am thankful for multiple conversations with Randal Jelks, an astute and passionate advocate for Hughes. David J. Garrow has been the most dedicated of scholars, generously helping me clarify my queries into Hughes's connections to Martin Luther King, Jr. Colleagues David Cecelski, Barbara Foley, and William J. Maxwell have likewise produced essential scholarship and personal insights concerning history, communism and the FBI. In addition to the continued support of Dean Jeffery Braden, my Department Head Antony Harrison kindly provided an off-campus scholarly assignment for me at just the right time to begin drafting this material.

Danny Glover's stirring 2016 performance of Langston Hughes's poetry at NC State University reminded me that Hughes's works needed to be heard. I was likewise moved to think of Hughes in new ways by listening to Ron Mccurdy's musical setting of *Ask Your Mamma* in Durham, North Carolina, in 2018. I am proudly informed precisely how Hughes's works continue to live on stage because Melissa Zeph and the Justice Theater Project mount *Black Nativity* on my campus every December. Friends at Busboys and Poets effectively highlight Hughes's focus on justice in the Washington, DC area. I applaud owner (and Hughes expert) Andy Shallal and programme organizer Olivia Jablonski for their civic work and the rewarding experience of sharing my scholarship at the historic Wardman Park Hotel.

I thank Vivian Constantinopoulos, Amy Salter and their entire team at Reaktion Books for editing and preparing this work. Megan Myers conducted early proofreading, and Austin Miller astutely prepared references once he learned no index was required. In addition to Kelsey Virginia Downs Dufresne, students in my autumn 2018 graduate seminar on Langston Hughes offered uncommon insights into the Harlem Renaissance, visual rhetoric, the Black Arts Movement, film, politics and Jesse B. Simple. Some of those students include William Christy, Jessica Dionne, Samantha Duke, Donato Fhunsu, Jay Irwin, Victoria Lambert, Travis Merchant, Brandy Reeves and Bridget Sharlow. My wife Sherri once again provided support and expertise in more ways than I can list. While such thanks is best expressed in person rather than ink, I ask she please remember there is a halo waiting for her somewhere.

Permissions

Photo Acknowledgements

The author and the publishers wish to express their thanks to the below sources of illustrative material and/or permission to reproduce it:

Beinecke Rare Book and Manuscript Library, Yale University, New Haven, CT, the James Weldon Johnson Collection: pp. 6, 11, 12, 13, 16, 19, 20, 23, 39, 53, 67, 70, 73, 76, 77, 78, 87, 88, 98 (Photo: Gordon Parks), 114, 120, 121, 133, 144, 179, 180, 187; the Wilson Library, University of North Carolina at Chapel Hill, Southern Historical Collection: pp. 34, 43, 60, 62.